WORLD BOOK'S
YOUNG SCIENTIST

WORLD BOOK'S

YOUNG SCIENTIST

Volume 9

World Book, Inc.
a Scott Fetzer company
Chicago   London   Sydney   Toronto

Activities that have this warning symbol require some adult supervision!

The quest to explore the known world and to describe its creation and subsequent development is nearly as old as mankind. In the Western world, the best-known creation story comes from the book of Genesis. It tells how God created the earth and all living things. Modern religious thinkers interpret the Biblical story of creation in various ways. Some believe that creation occurred exactly as Genesis describes it. Others think that God's method of creation is revealed through scientific investigation. *Young Scientist* presents an exciting picture of what scientists have learned about life and the universe.

World Book, Inc.
525 W. Monroe
Chicago, IL 60661

ISBN: 0-7166-2795-7
Library of Congress Catalog Card No. 94-68037

Printed in the United States of America

8 9 10 11 12 99 98 97 96 95 94

Contents

8 **Introducing structures**
All around us are structures, natural and artificial. Take a look at some examples.

10 **The shapes in structures**
Most structures are made from five simple shapes. Find shapes in a make-believe city.

12 **Choosing materials**
which materials are used for building? Test a collection of different materials.

14 **Structures that contain**
Special clothing protects racing drivers and football players. What job must containers do?

16 **The tug-of-war**
Why are ropes made of strong materials? Find out about tension and compression.

18 **Building materials**
Look at old and new buildings in different parts of the world. What are they made of?

20 **Building with bricks**
What are bricks made of? How are they used? Build a wall and test its strength.

22 **Sand and cement**
How are cement and concrete made? What prevents concrete from cracking?

24 **Reinforcing structures**
There are many ways of making structures stronger. Find out how reinforcing works.

26 **A steel frame**
How is steel made and used? What are the problems of building with steel?

28 **Building the first structures**
How did people build pyramids and temples thousands of years ago?

30 **Plans and models**
What does an architect do? Take a close look at a ground plan and an elevation.

32 **Firm foundations**
What keeps structures upright and in one place? Find out about foundations.

34 **Bridges**
Look at some early and simple examples of bridges. How are modern bridges built?

36 **Modern bridges**
Find out about three ways of building bridges with modern materials.

38 **Lattice towers**
What makes cranes and pylons so strong? Build a model lattice tower.

40 **Oil platforms**
Do you know how an oil platform is built and fixed to the seabed?

42 **Skyscrapers**
How are skyscrapers built? Why are steel and concrete used in skyscrapers?

44 **Hollow towers**
Why are space rockets and lighthouses so strong? Have a tower-building competition.

46 **Tunnels**
Building tunnels is dangerous and difficult. What will the Channel Tunnel look like?

48 **The strength of a dome**
Why don't domes collapse? Test a dome made from an eggshell. What is a geodesic dome?

50 **Holding back water**
What do different kinds of dams look like? Dams help to store water and to make energy.

52 **Roads**
Why are roads so important? How are roads designed and built?

54 **Under your feet**
What lies under the street? How are underground pipes and cables repaired?

56 **Keeping out moisture**
What is rising moisture? Find out how to keep your home dry.

58 **Insulation**
How can we keep the heat in or out of our homes? Test some different materials.

60 **Structures in the future**
Scientists have designed an indoor city of the future. Could you live there?

64 **Making life easier**
Many machines help us with our work. They are made from six simple machines.

66 Perpetual motion
Is there a machine that will run forever? Find out about perpetual motion machines.

68 Forces in action
Machines need energy to work. They must overcome powerful forces to keep running.

70 Friction
Some machines have many moving parts. What happens when they rub together?

72 What is a lever?
A lever is a simple machine. How does a lever help us with our work?

74 A machine for war
The catapult was invented for war. Make a model catapult to find out how it worked.

76 Levers and strings — grand piano
Levers can help us to make music. Have you ever looked inside a grand piano?

78 Inclined planes and wedges
A slope doesn't seem like a machine, but it can help us to make work easier.

80 Screws are machines
What makes a screw a special type of machine?

82 Wheels and axles
Can you imagine a world without wheels? Wheels can be useful in all sorts of ways.

84 Cogs, gears, and wheels
What are the moving parts inside a clock?

86 On two wheels
A bicycle is made up of many different machines. Find out what each machine does.

88 Pulleys — simple and complex
How can you use a wheel to lift a heavy weight? Build your own pulley.

90 Driving machines with energy
Machines cannot work without energy. Where does this energy come from?

92 Getting up steam
How does a steam locomotive work? Steam provides energy to drive the train's wheels.

94 What is a turbine?
Turbines can drive ships, jet airplanes, and electric generators.

96 Piston power
How does a piston engine work?

98 The automobile
Many different machines work together to make an automobile.

100 Pumping gas
Have you ever wondered where the gas comes from in a gas pump?

102 Reaching the fire
Fire-fighting machines can reach to the top of a high building. What are hydraulics?

104 A machine that flies
Imagine you are sitting at the controls of an airplane. How would you fly the plane?

106 Going up?
The quickest way to travel to the top of a building is in an elevator. How does an elevator work?

108 Electric motors
Can you find some small machines at home? Many will have an electric motor.

110 Printing revolution
Books used to be copied by hand. Now machines print many pages in a minute.

112 Machines to make machines
Machines are made up from many different parts. Each part must fit with the next.

114 Working on the assembly line
Special robot machines can build cars and help us with many other tasks.

116 Make a robot
Build your own robot using simple machines.

118 Glossary

120 Index

CONSTRUCTION

Introducing structures

Many animals make nests or other places in which to live. Birds make nests where they lay eggs and care for their young. Earthworms and badgers make burrows down in the ground. Some animals, like snails and shellfish, grow shells around themselves. The shells protect their soft bodies from predators.

Safe inside

Nests and burrows are **structures** made by animals. Shells are also structures. Animals can fit inside these structures, so we say they are structures that **enclose**. Human beings also make structures that enclose. Instead of nests, human beings build houses, offices, and factories. Instead of burrows, human beings build huge tunnels and underground shelters.

Support and span

Structures can **support** as well as enclose. The stem of a plant supports a flower in the same way that a lamppost supports a light, or a tall pillar supports a statue.

A spider's web is a structure that can **span** across the space between two twigs. And we build bridges that can span from one side of a river to the other.

The right materials

Animals use natural materials to build their structures. To build our structures we use natural materials, too, but scientists and engineers have made and discovered thousands of new materials. This means that structures made by human beings can be very large and complicated. Many human-made structures are patterned after natural designs.

Natural structures

Structures that enclose

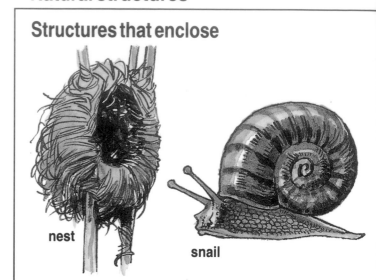

nest

snail

Structures that support

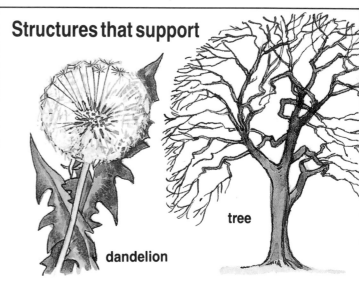

tree

dandelion

Structures that span

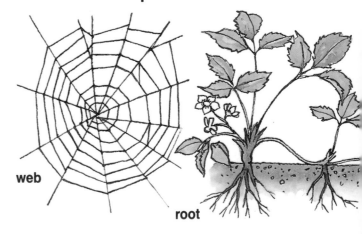

web

root

Human-made structures

wall

tent

house

tunnel

pillars

lamppost

scaffold

bench

crane

aqueduct

railway bridge

The shapes in structures

How many different structures can you think of ? There are natural structures like caves, skeletons, and trees. And there are also human-made structures like houses, bridges, and space rockets. These structures have very different shapes, but they all enclose, span, or support other things.

A whole structure like a tree or an airplane may appear to be very complicated. But complicated structures are made of smaller parts which are usually simple. In fact, most structures can be made from just five important and very simple shapes. These are sheets, cylinders, cubes, spheres, and cones.

Five simple shapes

You can make these shapes out of modeling clay and then use several together to make structures that are more complicated.

These shapes can be sliced in half, or cut smaller, to make other shapes.

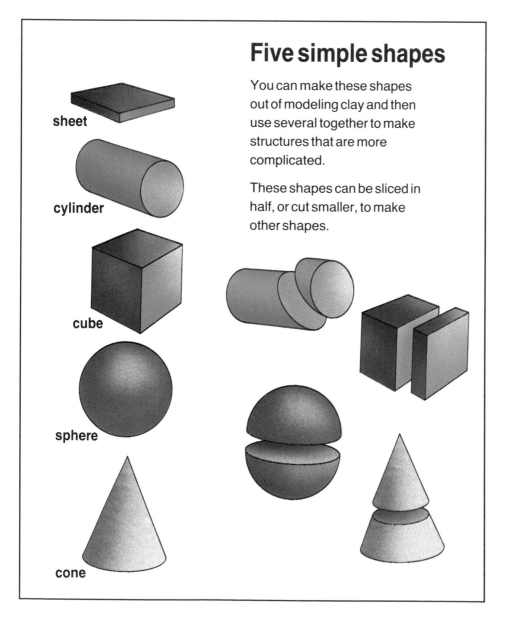

sheet

cylinder

cube

sphere

cone

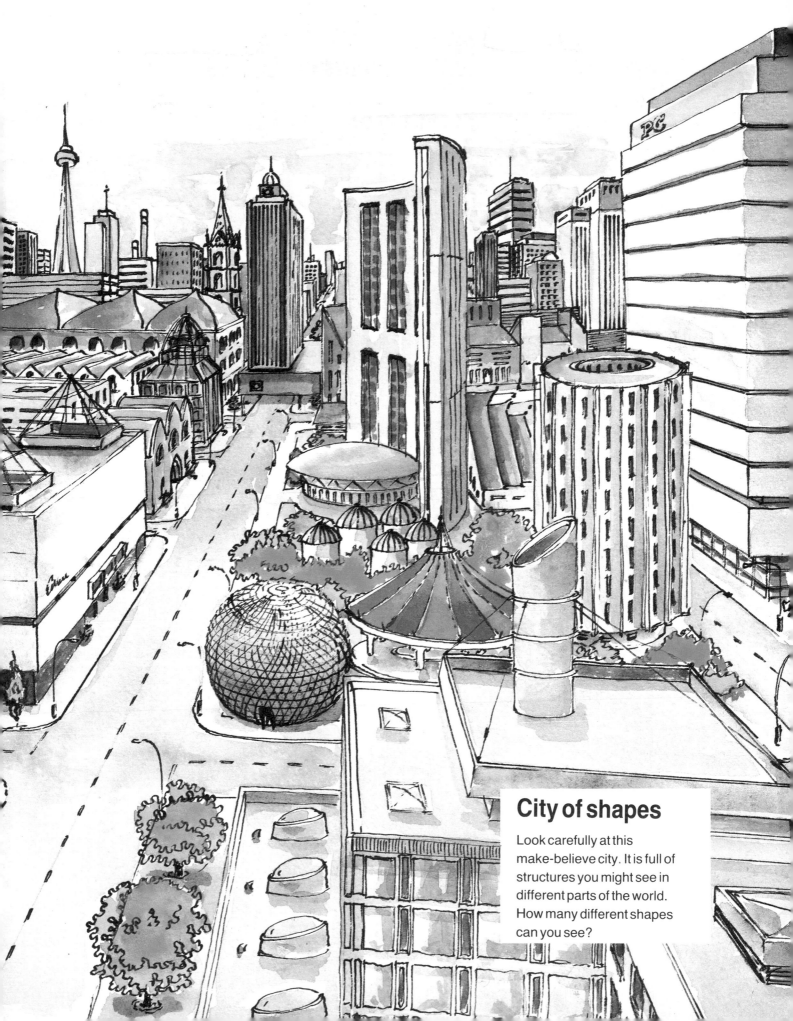

City of shapes

Look carefully at this make-believe city. It is full of structures you might see in different parts of the world. How many different shapes can you see?

Choosing materials

There are thousands of different materials in the world and many of them are useful for building structures. There are **natural** materials like wood, stone, cotton, and leather. There are also **artificial** materials like concrete, steel, glass, and plastics.

The right material for the job

Different structures are made from different materials. We must choose the right materials when making a new structure or it will not work properly. The body of an airplane is covered in light aluminum metal. If the body were covered in heavy steel, the airplane could never take off from the ground. But tough steel, and not soft aluminum is used to make bridges. An aluminum bridge would sag under the weight of traffic.

This airplane has a steel body. What do you think will happen when the pilot tries to fly the plane?

This aluminum bridge is heavy with traffic. What is happening to it?

How materials behave

To choose the right materials for each structure, we need to know how a material will behave if it is used in a certain way. We need to know the **properties** of a material. Is it hard or soft? Does it stretch or bend easily? How does it react to heat or water? How heavy is it compared with other materials? You can discover more by making a collection of different materials. Sort your materials into two groups—natural and artificial—and then test their properties.

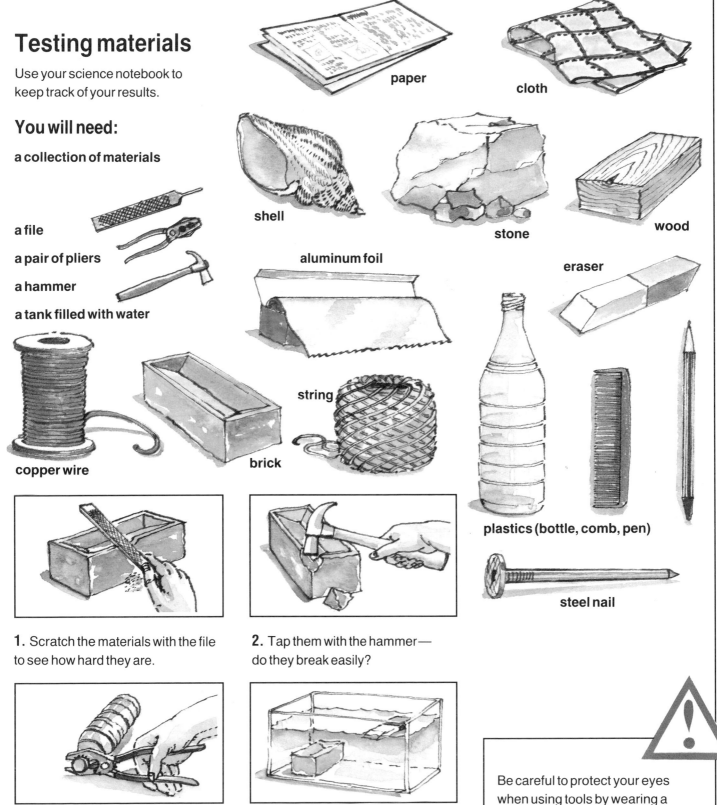

Testing materials

Use your science notebook to keep track of your results.

You will need:

a collection of materials

a file

a pair of pliers

a hammer

a tank filled with water

paper

cloth

shell

stone

wood

aluminum foil

eraser

copper wire

brick

string

plastics (bottle, comb, pen)

steel nail

1. Scratch the materials with the file to see how hard they are.

2. Tap them with the hammer— do they break easily?

3. Squeeze them with the pliers to see if they are bendable.

4. Do they float or sink when they are dropped into water?

Be careful to protect your eyes when using tools by wearing a pair of safety glasses. Adult supervision is recommended.

Structures that contain

Think of all the sports you know that are fun to watch. Some of the most enjoyable are the fastest. They can also be dangerous! A racing driver or a football player, even a hockey player, can finish a race or a game with bad bumps and bruises. For this reason, many athletes must wear special clothing to protect themselves.

This clothing is specially designed for the job it must do. The racing driver wears a helmet to protect the head from injury. It is made of tough fiberglass so it won't crack. It is padded to absorb any bumps and knocks. The hockey player may wear special gloves, leg pads, or a face shield, and the football player also pads his shoulders and thighs.

The helmet, the gloves, and the shoulder pads are protective **containers.** They do the same kind of job as the soft cardboard container that protects eggs, the aluminum container that encloses a soft drink, or the see-through plastic container that protects a new shirt.

These sportspeople must protect themselves from injury. They wear helmets and padded clothing.

hockey player　　**football player**　　**racing driver**

These bottles are different shapes and are made from different materials. They are all designed to contain liquids.

Shape and size

Containers are types of structures. Just like any other structure, a container must be designed to do its job. It may need to protect a driver's skull, hold a liquid, or enclose a solid shape. It may need to be stiff or bendable, to be heavy or light, waterproof or watertight. And like all structures, containers are made of many different materials.

Which materials?

The material used for the container depends on its contents, too. You can't store water in a paper bag. The material must be strong enough, or strengthened, to support the weight of the contents. But it must be light enough for us to carry.

The tug-of-war

"Heave! Heave!" Each tug-of-war team is trying to pull the rope in its direction. The tiny ribbon tied at the center of the rope moves a few inches in one direction, but then, as the losing team digs in its heels, it creeps a few inches back. Four people are pulling at each end of the rope. The rope must take all the **tension** of being pulled in both directions. Tension is a force that tries to pull things apart.

The rope has been made so that it will not break. We say the rope has high **tensile strength,** because it can withstand the forces trying to pull it apart.

Tension and compression

The opposite of tension is **compression,** which is a force that tries to crush things. Cars and trucks push down on a bridge and compress the foundations. Bridges must be made from materials that do not easily collapse.

Both teams are pulling with all their strength. There is tension in the rope in both directions. The rope must be strong, or else it will break.

Equal forces

Whatever part of a structure is required to support the force of a pull or a push or a heavy weight, there must be an equal force pushing or pulling in the opposite direction. Where the forces of tension and compression are not equal, the structure will bend or collapse.

This building in France stays up because its cables keep the forces of tension and compression equal. If one cable broke, the forces would become unequal and part of the building might collapse.

Building materials

The first structures were made of materials that people could find easily where they lived. All the buildings in one area often looked similar. Today, buildings are made of lots of different materials. The next time you visit a city, look at the buildings and see what different materials you can identify.

This building is made of red sandstone and marble. It was built more than 400 years ago, in Delhi, India.

The walls of these log cabins are made from tree trunks. The roofs are made of wooden tiles. The houses can be made quickly and fairly easily.

Structures in stone

Stone is a very strong material to use. But it is difficult to work with and heavy to move. Because it is so strong, stone is often used for important structures, which are designed to last.

Structures in wood

Wood is easy to cut and shape. It can be tied or nailed together to make frames, and sawed into strips to make outside walls. Almost any kind of wood can be used to build a simple house.

Things we can use

In many countries today, housebuilders still use the materials that they can find most easily. In some places, these materials may even be flattened cans, pieces of plastic, or parts of wooden boxes.

Modern materials

Many of the materials we use for building today are artificial. Steel and concrete help us to build taller and taller buildings. Specially strengthened glass can be used as well. Most parts of a structure are now made in a factory and then put together at the building site.

This house in the West Indies is made of many different materials. How many can you identify?

Some new buildings are covered with plastic panels strengthened with fiberglass.

Building with bricks

The first people who settled in one place and built homes for themselves chose river valleys where there was a good water supply for farming. People found that the mud on the river banks made a good building material if it was molded into blocks and dried. These were the first **bricks.**

Today's bricks are often made of **clay.** Clay is rock that has been broken down over thousands of years into tiny particles. When the clay has been cut, it must be "worked" in the same way as dough is kneaded before making bread. "Working" used to be done by the feet of workers in the fields where the clay was cut, but today it is done by machine. Shale is also often used to make bricks.

When most of the water has been squeezed out, the clay is punched through a hole that molds it into the shape of a brick. As it comes out, it is trimmed, and the bricks are stacked to dry. Then they are baked in ovens or kilns until they are hard.

In this wall, the bricks are stacked on top of each other.

In this wall, the bricks overlap. Which wall is stronger?

Blow the wall down

You will need:

building blocks

a ball

Use building blocks from your box of toys to make copies of the two walls. Test which wall is the most difficult to push over. Try blowing them over. Try rolling a ball against each one.

Hampton Court, near London, England, is a brick palace built nearly 500 years ago.

Bricks are small and light enough for one person to work with. Walls that will not be seen once a building is finished are often made of larger blocks, which can be laid faster.

Find out more by looking at pages **14–15**
16–17

Sand and cement

If you want to join two pieces of paper or cardboard, you use glue to bind the separate pieces together. The bricklayer's "glue" is a mixture of cement, sand, and water called **mortar.** When mortar dries, it becomes hard and holds the bricks together.

Cement is a very important building material. The ancient Romans developed a kind of cement similar to the kinds used today. Cement is made by mixing lime and clay with water, drying the mixture, and then burning it. This makes a kind of cake called **clinker,** which is then ground to a fine powder.

Cement forms crystals when water is added to it. The crystals grow and cling to each other. When the cement dries, the crystals stay locked together. If cement is mixed with sand to make mortar, the cement crystals lock around the grains of sand as well.

Mixing concrete

Cement is also used to make **concrete.** This is a mixture of cement, sand, water, and small stones. As concrete dries, it hardens, and the cement crystals hold the sand and stones in place. While concrete is still wet, it can be poured into molds, to harden into any shape.

Concrete is used in many different kinds of structures. Roads and sidewalks can be made from it. It is often used for the foundations of buildings and for basement floors. When it is used on bridges and buildings, its surface is sometimes marked in squares so that it looks like blocks of stone. Concrete is also used for building dams, harbor walls, and breakwaters.

Giant strength!

If you were a very strong giant and tried to bend a slab of concrete, what do you think would happen? The top of the slab would be compressed. It would be under compression. The bottom of the slab would be under tension. Concrete cannot withstand tension because it cannot stretch, so the bottom of the slab would crack.

This slab of concrete would crack very easily if the giant bent it this much.

Concrete takes the strain

The forces acting on a concrete beam produce stresses in the concrete. Tension tries to stretch it. Compression presses the concrete together and tries to crush it. Concrete can easily withstand compression forces. But it needs extra strength to withstand tension, because it cracks easily.

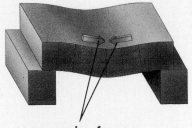

compression forces

When concrete beams are used to carry the gigantic weight of a heavy structure, they are strengthened with rods or bars. This is called **reinforced concrete.** The steel rods or bars resist the tension and keep the bottom of the beam from cracking. Often, the rods are arranged in a grid pattern.

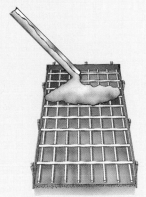

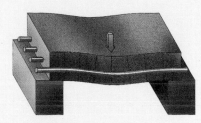

reinforced concrete

Prestressed concrete is reinforced, but in a special way. Steel cables are held stretched while the concrete hardens around them. When the concrete is hard, the steel cables are released and compress the concrete. This gives it extra strength. Prestressed concrete beams can support heavier loads than ordinary reinforced concrete.

prestressed concrete

Gladesville Bridge in Sydney, Australia, was built from prestressed concrete. It was made in sections and then put together across the river.

Reinforcing structures

Steel is strong. The bodies of many cars, trucks, and ships are made from sheets of steel fastened together. But steel is a very heavy metal, so the sheets must be rolled as thin as possible. Car bodies may be made from sheets of steel that are so thin that you could even bend them with your bare hands. So why don't cars bend and sag as you step inside them? The answer is that the sheets of steel are **reinforced.**

Reinforcing makes cars, trucks, and ships stronger. The sheets of steel are bent into special shapes to strengthen them. Extra pieces of metal are also fastened to them to make each sheet stronger.

Reinforcing at work

You can see how reinforcing works by trying some experiments with cardboard.

You will need:

three strips of cardboard, each 4 in (10 cm) x 8 in (20 cm)

two smaller strips of cardboard, each 2 in (5 cm) x 4 in (10 cm)

two books, each about 2 in (5 cm) thick

a handful of coins, all the same size

a ruler

a pencil

a blunt knife

glue

1. Place the books 4 inches (10 centimeters) apart on the table and span the gap with a large piece of cardboard. Now load the cardboard with coins in the middle, until it sags so much that it just touches the table. Note your results.

2. Use the ruler and pencil to draw lines down the length of another piece of cardboard ½ inch (1.25 centimeters) apart. Using the blunt knife, score the cardboard along the lines. Make V-shaped folds in it. Span the gap again and load the cardboard with coins until it sags and touches the table. Does it carry more or fewer coins than the first cardboard?

3. Make both the smaller pieces of cardboard into two separate U shapes. Use glue to attach these under the third large piece of cardboard. Span the gap and load the cardboard with coins again until it sags. Describe the strength of this structure.

spiral staircase

Propping things up

Some very large trees in the rain forest grow structures called **buttresses** to reinforce their trunks. This helps to keep the trunks straight and to prevent the enormous trees from collapsing. Large buildings can have stone buttresses to reinforce tall walls.

buttress on a building

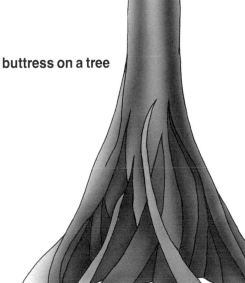

buttress on a tree

nautilus shell

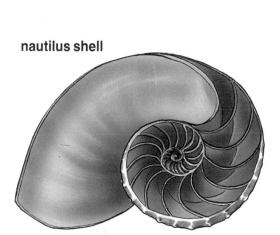

Winding around

The nautilus shell is home to a small sea animal. The animal increases the size of its shell by growing new sections at the outer edge. The shell grows in a spiral and makes a strong home. Any force on it is spread outwards from the central ring. Spiral staircases are stronger than ones that drop, without supports, straight down to the ground. The strength is in the curved, winding shape.

A steel frame

Hidden behind the outside walls of many large, modern structures is a **framework** of columns and beams. In the early days of framework construction, iron was sometimes used for the framework. But steel proved to be more durable and adaptable. Most of the famous skyscrapers in New York City were built on steel frames. Today, prestressed concrete can also be used for long bridges and medium-sized buildings.

Structural engineers design the framework of a building. They choose the type of steel to be used and decide how the framework will fit together. Most of the steel parts, such as beams and girders, are joined together before being fitted into the whole framework.

Problems with steel

One of the great dangers in a building is fire. When steel is hot, it expands and swells up. In a serious fire, the steel framework could lose its strength, and the building could come crashing down. For this reason, steel frames are often covered in concrete or other material to protect them from fierce heat.

Bridges made of steel are sometimes hinged so that they can move slightly. This allows the steel to expand safely in hot weather without damaging the structure.

Another danger to steel structures is rust caused by wet weather and pollution in the atmosphere. This is one reason why steel used in new structures is rarely open to the air.

The Statue of Liberty stands on an island in New York Harbor. The outer casing is made of sheets of copper. Inside, there is a strong frame made of iron and stainless steel.

The framework of the Statue of Liberty is made of iron and steel.

Making steel

Steel is made by heating and purifying iron. Most steel beams for building are shaped by a process called **rolling.** Red-hot steel is squeezed between rollers, which form it into different shapes. These shapes are designed to make beams stronger and better able to stand up to the forces of compression and tension.

Girders are lowered into position to form the frame of a large office building.

Building the first structures

Bulldozers, excavators, tower cranes, pile-drivers, trench-diggers—just think of all the machinery on a big building site! It is hard to think of large structures being built without powerful machines. But they were.

The people of Babylon, who lived almost 4,000 years ago, built tall temples called *ziggurats*. The ancient Egyptians built pyramids and great palaces for their kings. In Britain and France, people made huge circles of stone. Later, in Mexico, the Aztecs built temples to worship their sun god.

How did they do it?

None of these ancient peoples had powerful machinery to help them. So they relied on the muscle power of workers to dig, lift, and drag. They dragged the huge blocks of stone on sleds or rollers to make them easier to move. When they got to the building site, they could use levers to raise the stones into position. Ramps were built so that the blocks could be dragged higher up the structure.

They probably had no instruments to help them check that a site was level. So the builders of the Egyptian pyramids dug trenches on the site and filled them with water. The water found its own level and showed up any bumps or hollows. The engineers at the time had their own ways to solve the problems that all builders face.

As the pyramid grew higher, ramps of mud and small rocks were built so that stone could be hauled up to continue building.

In ancient Egypt, the builders of the pyramids used the muscle power of gangs of workers to build these immense structures.

A test of skill

The Aztecs of Mexico built their temples on pyramids. These people probably knew nothing about how the ancient Egyptians built their pyramids, and so the Aztecs had to solve their building problems for themselves. Some of these problems were so complicated that they would test the skills of engineers and architects even today.

The ancient city of Teotihuacán in Mexico was destroyed by Chichimec Indian tribes about 1,100 years ago.

The ancient Chinese built the Great Wall to keep out invaders from the north. It is the longest structure ever built, nearly 4,000 miles (6,400 kilometers) long.

Stonehenge in England is a huge stone circle. It may have been a religious center. Building began about 2800 B.C. Some of the stones are nearly 23 feet (7 meters) high.

The Great Stupa at Sanchi, in central India, is a temple of the Buddhist religion built more than 2,000 years ago.

Plans and models

An **architect** is employed to design a building. The building may be a home, an office, or a factory. The design and structure should be adapted to the use of the building. It must provide for all the inhabitants and their belongings, as well as their special needs. The building should also look good.

The architect makes a **scale drawing** or a **scale model** of the design to show what the building will look like. In a scale drawing or model, the building looks as if it has shrunk. Individual parts are in the same proportion to each other as they will be when the building is finished. If the building is to be a large structure, such as a bridge or an office block, the architect will work with a **structural engineer.** The engineer will decide what shape and strength the framework will be, whether the building will be strong enough, and how the engineering problems are to be solved.

This house is in Melbourne, Australia. Try to compare the house with the drawings opposite.

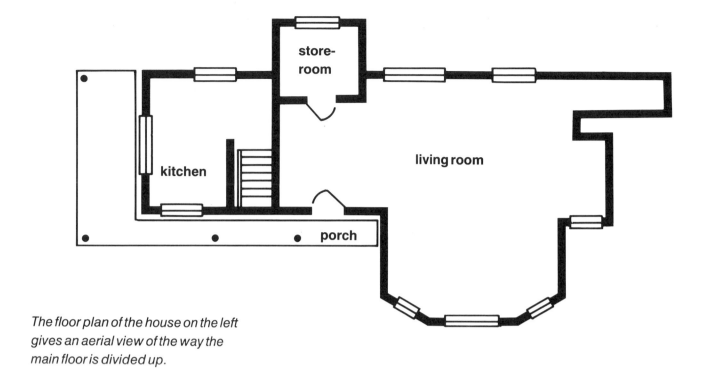

The floor plan of the house on the left gives an aerial view of the way the main floor is divided up.

A different way of looking

The layout of a building can be seen in its **plans.** The **floor plans** give an aerial, or bird's-eye, view of each room and each story. They show every room as well as the corridors and stairways, with the position of every door and window carefully marked. **Elevations** are plans that show what each outside wall will look like.

The plans drawn on this page are plans of the house in the photograph. Do you think they look like the house?

The elevation shows what each side of the house looks like. This elevation shows the front of the house.

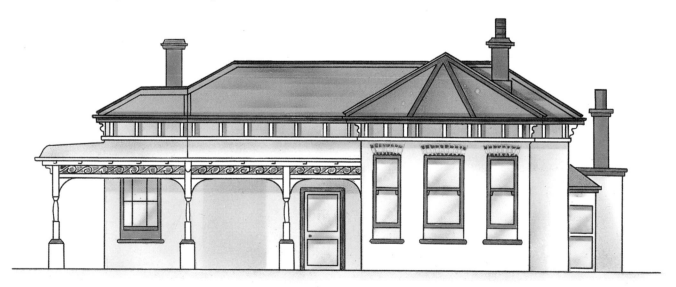

Firm foundations

The first job in building any structure is to prepare the site where it will be built. The whole weight of a building will rest on its base, so the structure must have **foundations** that are very strong and will not move.

The engineer first has to find out what kind of soil or rock is under the site. A special tool called a **bore** is drilled down into the ground. It collects a **core** made up of samples of all the layers of soil and rock it passes through. This tells the engineer what lies underground.

Types of foundations

Different kinds of foundations are used to support a structure, depending on the kind of ground it will rest on.

*If there is rock close to the surface, a **pier foundation** can be built directly on to it.*

*A **mat** or **raft foundation** of thick concrete laid under a building spreads out its weight.*

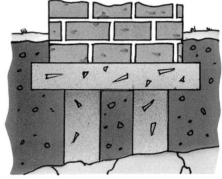

*On soft ground, steel or concrete columns form a **pile foundation** that carries a structure's weight down to solid rock.*

Testing foundations

If a structure has a strong, firm base, it will be much more stable. You can see in this experiment how stability is important.

You will need:

an empty, transparent plastic bottle

water

1. Stand the bottle on a table. Try to blow it over. You will not need to blow very hard.

2. Add 1 inch (2.5 centimeters) of water and try again. Is your assignment more difficult?

3. See if you can find the exact amount of water you need in the bottle to keep you from blowing the bottle over.

Staying upright

A wall built on soft ground may fall over.

The foundations make sure that the wall remains stable.

The foundations of the Leaning Tower of Pisa in Italy are unable to support the tower evenly. The tower leans by more than 14.5 feet (4.4 meters). The ground underneath it is still sinking very slowly.

Bridges

Bridges allow people to cross obstacles such as rivers, canyons, and busy roads and railways. Bridges were among the first structures ever built. As soon as people began to travel, they found that they needed to cross rivers. The science of bridge-building goes back thousands of years. But new ways of building bridges, using new materials, are still being found.

There are many different ways in which a bridge can be built. The design will depend on the answers to many questions. How wide is the river? How long will the bridge need to be? How fast does the river flow? Will there be sudden floods? Are there strong winds? What loads will it have to carry? What kind of rock or soil will be under the foundations?

Span bridge

The **span bridge** is the simplest and earliest kind of bridge. The first ones were probably tree trunks supported by the river bank at each end. Later, more tree trunks would be added side by side, and planks laid across them to make a flat surface. Such a surface is easier to walk across. These bridges may be supported by piers, so that they are higher than the water even when the river is flooded.

The Pont du Gard in southern France was built by the ancient Romans. It is an aqueduct, which is a bridge built to carry water. The water is carried 160 feet (48 meters) above the valley floor.

This simple wooden bridge in Malaysia was built high enough that people can cross the river even when it is flooded.

Arch bridge

Arch bridges were first built over 4,000 years ago, by the Babylonians. The earliest ones had many arches to support a roadway or canal. Later, stronger arches were developed that could be more widely spaced.

The ancient Romans built their arch bridges in brick or stone. The bricks were normally wedge-shaped and placed in the arch shape so that each brick pressed against the ones on either side of it. The keystone was a large, central brick, which fitted into the center of the arch. As a heavy load passes over the bridge, its weight is spread across the rounded arch.

Girder bridge

Modern span bridges are called **girder bridges.** They are straight spans and the ends of the girders may be supported by a pier or abutment. The material used for the span may have to be reinforced to support the weight it will carry. In one type, the **box girder bridge,** each girder looks like a long, hollow box that lies between the piers. This shape gives a greater strength to the bridge than does a simple girder.

This girder bridge crosses the Nile at Omdurman in Sudan. The arched sides give it extra strength.

This cable-stayed bridge has only one cable attaching the road to the tower. Some bridges have more cables.

The Verrazano Narrows suspension bridge crosses the entrance to New York Harbor. It was the longest suspension bridge in the world when it was built in 1964.

The Firth of Forth railway bridge in Scotland was the first large cantilever bridge. It was built in 1890, and it is still one of the largest in the world.

Modern bridges

There are three types of bridges designed and built today. These are the **cantilever bridge,** the **suspension bridge,** and the **cable-stayed bridge.**

Cantilever bridge

A cantilever bridge is a type of span bridge. It has two beams, or cantilevers, each resting on a pier, with a shorter central section joining them. One end of each cantilever is connected to the river bank by the anchor arm. This stretches from the pier to the bank. The cantilever arm stretches from the pier to the other end of the cantilever and supports the central section. A cantilever bridge can also have more than two cantilevers. Long cantilever bridges are built with steel, which is light and very strong.

Suspension bridge

Suspension bridges have steel cables stretching from one end to the other, passing over high towers. More cables connect the main cables to the bridge deck and carry the weight upwards. Suspension bridges use very few materials and can span great distances. The roadways on these bridges are often reinforced to prevent them from twisting and cracking in the wind.

Cable-stayed bridge

Cable-stayed bridges are a mixture of the span and suspension types. Cables from the road are connected directly to the towers.

The Eiffel Tower was built as the main attraction of the Paris Exhibition of 1889. Notice all the triangles formed in the structure. This is a lattice tower.

Test the shapes

First find which lattice shape is the most rigid.

You will need:

drinking straws cut into 4¼-in (10.6-cm) and 6-in (15-cm) lengths

modeling clay

Lattice towers

Do you know what the arm of a crane and an electrical pylon have in common? They are both very long and made of thin strips of steel. They are also extremely strong. The arm of a crane helps to lift heavy loads. Pylons hold huge lengths of electrical cable high up in the air. Both these structures are called **lattice** structures, and they are made from thin strips of steel joined together in a special pattern. A lattice structure is created when the horizontal and vertical sides of a metal cage are strengthened by diagonal bars. These strengthen the sides and keep the cage from bending. They make it more rigid. There are several ways of arranging the diagonal bars, but the shape that gives the greatest strength is the triangular shape.

Building a radio mast

Lattice masts made from steel are often used to hold up radio transmitting antennas. Some are more than 330 feet (100 meters) tall. Most have three long pieces of steel arranged in a triangle to make the sides. These are held together by smaller lengths of steel arranged in triangular patterns. The mast does not fall over because guy wires stretch from the mast to the ground—making more triangular shapes!

Try making a model lattice mast from plastic drinking straws. Now that you know the secret of the design, you should easily manage to make a model tower as much as 40 inches (1 meter) high.

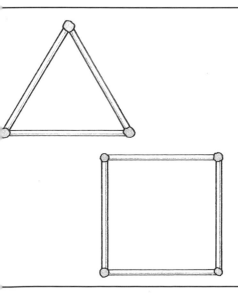

1. Join three pieces of the drinking straws with modeling clay to make a triangle. Then make a square from four pieces of straw.

2. Lay the square and the triangle on the table and squeeze them to see which one holds its shape best.

You will find that the corners of the square are easily bent. The triangle has only three sides and the corners do not bend easily

Strengthen the cage

Try a second experiment to test the strength of triangles.

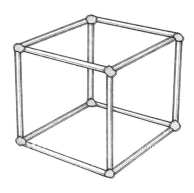

1. Use straws to make a cube out of squares. Stand the cube on a table and place your hand on top. It will be easy to squash the cube flat.

Where might you add extra straws to make the cube more rigid?

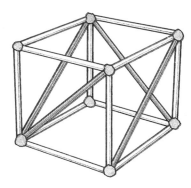

2. Use the longer pieces of the drinking straws to join opposite corners of each of the square's sides. This adds triangles to the cube and helps it to keep its shape when you push it down.

Oil platforms

Structures at sea have to stand up to great forces. Hurricane force winds may blow around them. Waves may crash against them. Strong currents under the water may cause movements in the seabed.

Oil platforms stand far out at sea and pump oil up from the ground beneath. They are among the largest constructions ever built. Some are built on structures that go down 1,000 feet (300 meters) or more into the water. Most platforms are made of steel. The steel structure under the water that supports the **deck,** or working area, is called the **jacket.** The jacket is a spider's web of steel tubes joined together to make a strong lattice framework. The pipes that bring up the oil fit inside it.

Moving oil platforms

The jacket is built on its side. When it is finished, tugs tow it, floating on air tanks, to its site out at sea. The tanks are slowly filled with water, and the jacket tilts until it is upright. Huge steel legs are than driven into the seabed to hold the platform in place. Sometimes concrete legs are used.

Sometimes a **semisubmersible** platform is used. This floats on the surface, buoyed up by vast tanks filled with air. It is firmly anchored to the seabed with steel cables. A semisubmersible platform is normally used for exploration and test drilling. It can be moved to a different site.

The platform is towed out to the drilling site by tugs.

Once in place, the platform usually stands about 83 feet (25 meters) above the surface of the sea.

concrete legs   **steel legs**   **steel cables**

Oil platforms can be fixed to the seabed in different ways. Some platforms have concrete legs used to store the oil. Others have long steel legs. Huge steel cables are also used to anchor oil platforms to the seabed.

Skyscrapers

About 6 million people live in Hong Kong, a tiny country on the coast of China. It fits into a very small space between the mountains and the sea. So people live in tall blocks of apartments, one family above another. These **skyscrapers,** as they are called, allow people to live and work together wherever space is limited. The cities of New York in the United States, Tokyo in Japan, and São Paulo in Brazil are all famous for their skyscrapers.

The first skyscraper was built about 100 years ago in Chicago, Illinois. It had only 10 floors but it was the first building to have a metal framework, made of iron and steel beams. The framework, and not the walls, supported the floors of the building. The use of steel was an important advance in building skyscrapers. Steel is stronger and lighter than iron. This makes it possible to build very tall structures. The steel framework is covered with panels called **cladding.**

The force of the wind

One of the problems that engineers face when designing a skyscraper is the strength of the wind. A skyscraper may sway in a strong wind, so it must be held in place by a strong frame and deep foundations.

Steel and concrete are the two most important materials used in building skyscrapers. Neither material is strong enough on its own to support the building, but steel is strong under tension, and concrete is strong under compression. Inside the steel framework is the **core.** This is a hollow, reinforced concrete rectangle. The core is the building's backbone or spine. It is very strong. Many of the services in the building, such as the elevators and the power supply, may be built into the core.

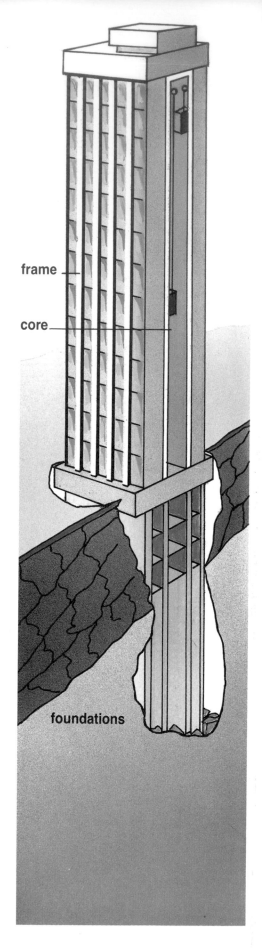

frame

core

foundations

Engineers can build stable skyscrapers over a hundred stories high by using a steel framework, a concrete core, and deep foundations.

Hong Kong's skyscrapers are used for offices, housing, and hotels.

Hollow towers

Street lamps, lighthouses, and space rockets—all these structures are made in the shape of hollow tubes, or cylinders. This shape is strong and difficult to crush or bend. Making hollow towers from cylinders also uses fewer materials than other structures of the same size.

Whose tower is the tallest?

Why not have a tower-building competition with your friends? Each person starts with the same amount of materials—just four sheets of cardboard, a pair of scissors, and some masking tape. You are trying to design and build the tallest tower that can stand by itself.

You will need:

four sheets of cardboard

scissors

masking tape

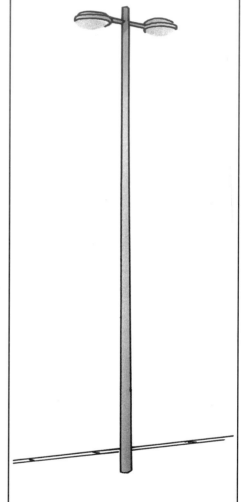

Street lamp

Street lamps are long, thin metal tubes with lights at the top. The bottom end of the tube is buried in the ground. This keeps the street lamp standing straight even when very strong winds blow.

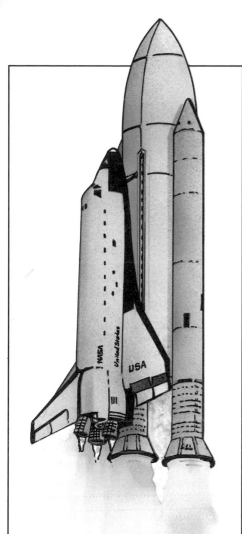

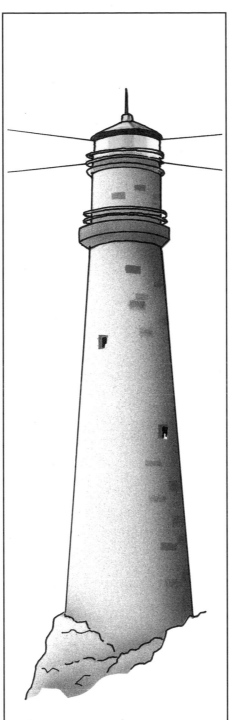

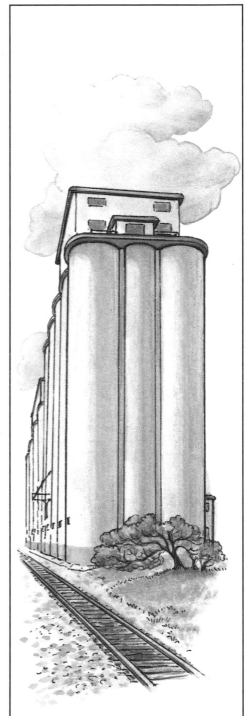

Space rocket

Space rockets are slim,
pointed cylinders that can
be over 233 feet (70 meters)
tall. The rocket must be light,
but strong enough to both
support the engines and fuel
tanks inside and escape from
the pull of earth's gravity.

Lighthouse

Lighthouses are towers that
are usually built from stone.
They must be tall so that their
light can be seen from far
away. Their circular shape
stands up well to the force
of the wind and waves.

Grain elevators

Grain elevators are towers that
load, unload, clean, mix, and
store grain. They are made of
concrete or steel, and may
stand more than 100 feet
(30 meters) high.

Tunnels

If you have ever been on a train or traveled across a big city, you have probably been inside a tunnel. Tunnels carry rail tracks and roads through hills and mountains or under rivers. Underground railways run in tunnels underneath many cities.

A tunnel is a special kind of structure. It must be deep underground, so that it does not damage the foundations of any buildings that stand above it. It has to stand up to the compression forces of the ground and buildings, or water, above. There must be a good drainage system to pump water away. Long tunnels need a supply of fresh air, which must be pumped through them from ventilation shafts.

Tunneling has always been very dangerous. There is the danger of sudden rock falls, or water rushing in. The Japanese have designed tunneling machines that require no underground operators. Everything is controlled from the surface, using lasers and closed-circuit television.

Joining France and Great Britain

In 1990 a group of tunnel workers from Great Britain shook hands with a group of tunnel workers from France, 57 yards (52 meters) below the seabed of the English Channel. In 1993, these two teams will complete the Channel Tunnel— one of the longest tunnels in the world.

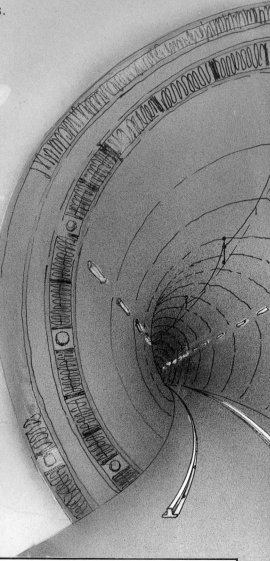

An underground railray runs underneath the city of London, England.

The Channel Tunnel will carry high-speed trains in two tunnels, which will flank a service tunnel.

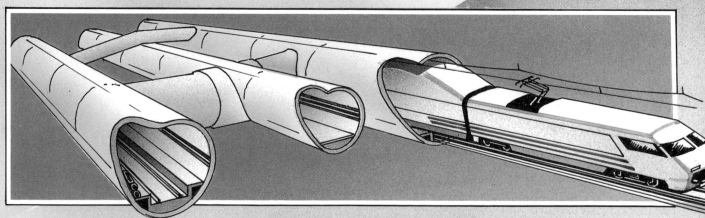

Digging deep

There are several ways of building a tunnel. These include the **cut and cover method, blasting,** and **boring.**

Cut and cover tunnels are built close to the surface. The first stage is to dig a trench down to the level of the tunnel floor. Reinforced concrete is used to build a floor, walls, and a roof. When the concrete has hardened, the trench is filled in again, up to street level.

Tunnels built through hard rock are usually blasted. Workers use explosives to blast each section of rock, and then they remove the broken pieces. Often the workers must build supports in each newly-opened portion of the tunnel to prevent weak rock from falling when the next section is blasted.

To tunnel through clay or soft rock, huge boring machines push a steel tube through the ground. These boring machines can be guided by satellite, by computer, and by laser to make sure the tunnels go in the right direction. Reinforced concrete or steel can be used to make the floor, walls, and roof of the tunnel.

This map shows the route of the new tunnel linking France and Great Britain. The tunnel is being built about 57 yards (52 meters) underneath the seabed.

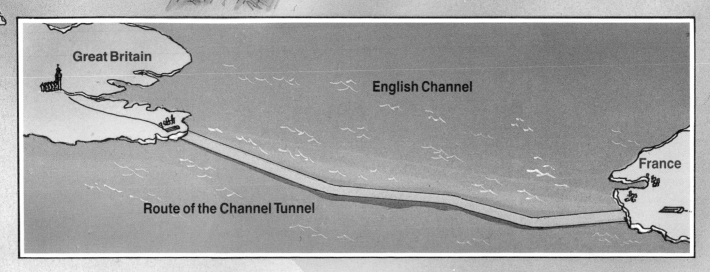

Great Britain

English Channel

France

Route of the Channel Tunnel

The strength of a dome

Have you ever turned the empty shell of a boiled egg upside down in the eggcup and tried to break it with a spoon? It is surprising to find how much force you need. The **dome** shape of the shell adds strength to the fragile material of the shell. The tension caused by the knock of your spoon is carried down the sides of the shell and into the eggcup. The tension is spread down the sloping sides of the structure.

Dome-shaped roofs are strong in exactly the same way. Architects have used them in buildings for many years. Two famous buildings, the Taj Mahal in India and the Capitol in the United States, have domes. Look for buildings with domes the next time you visit a city.

How strong is a dome?

You can see how strong eggshells are with this experiment.

You will need:

four empty eggshells

a small pair of scissors

masking tape

some books, all about the same size

2. Carefully cut around the eggshell through the masking tape, so that you have four eggshell halves with even bottoms.

1. Put a piece of masking tape around the middle of the eggshell. This will prevent the eggshell from cracking when you cut it.

3. Put the eggshells on the table, dome up, in a rectangle that's just a bit smaller than one of your books.

4. Put a book on the eggshells. Keep adding books until the eggshells crack. How many books can they support?

Geodesic domes

After World War II, an American architect, Richard Buckminster Fuller, came up with a new idea for a domed structure. He designed a dome-shaped frame made of triangles of steel rods. The circular base of the dome could rest on the ground or on columns. The triangular spaces were filled in with light panels.

This kind of structure is called a **geodesic dome.** Its curved shape makes it pleasing to look at. But it is most useful because it holds itself up. No extra supports are needed inside.

Most geodesic domes are built to last, but they are so easy to set up and take down that they are sometimes used only for a short time. They make good halls for exhibitions, concerts, and some sports events. A geodesic dome was erected in the Philippines in just 22 hours.

This is a photograph of a geodesic dome at Newcastle University in Great Britain.

You can build a model geodesic dome like the one shown above. You will need to cut 32 drinking straws in half and join the pieces together with modeling clay.

Holding back water

People have always found ways of making water work for them. In Babylon and ancient Egypt, people built **dams** to keep high river waters from flooding their farmland. Dams are also built across rivers to create bodies of water known as **reservoirs.** The dam stops the river from flowing, and a reservoir is created behind the dam. This provides water for the dry season.

The great weight of water held back by a dam pushes against the dam. This weight puts huge force, or **pressure,** on the dam. Some dams use this pressure to help change the water's energy to a form of energy that can be used. When gates in the dam are opened, powerful streams of water are released. The streams turn a turbine which drives a generator to make electricity. Electricity made in this way is called **hydroelectricity.**

Different kinds of dams

The earliest kind of dam was simply a bank of mud and rocks built across a river. Dams like this, called **embankment dams,** are in use all over the world. Today, they are often strengthened with a concrete core.

Embankment dams are sometimes not strong enough to hold back the weight of water stored in a modern reservoir. So stronger dams are built of concrete that has been reinforced with steel. Sometimes dams have thick concrete supports called buttresses to help hold back the weight of the water. These dams are called **buttress dams.** Many of the largest dams are built in the shape of an arch. The **arch dam** spreads the weight of the water to the land on each side. There are many arch dams in mountainous areas of North America.

The effect of a dam

An engineer must think about many things when planning a dam. The ground beneath the dam must be carefully checked to make sure that it can support the weight of the dam and the water. If a dam bursts, it would bring disaster to the area. The engineer must calculate how strong the dam must be to withstand the pressure of the water. The engineer must then make it even stronger, in case the water rises above its usual level or the wind whips the surface into strong waves.

The Hoover Dam, in Nevada, is a combination of an arch and an embankment dam. It is one of the tallest concrete dams in the world.

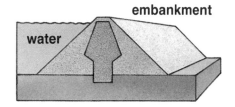

embankment

This embankment dam has a core of concrete.

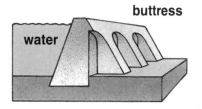

buttress

In this buttress dam, extra strength comes from the buttresses on the side away from the water.

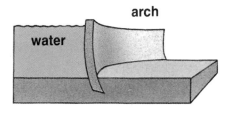

arch

Arch dams spread the weight of the water to the land on each side of the dam.

Roads

A network of roads allows cars to travel to most places in the country.

The streets in residential neighborhoods often have only one or two lanes for moving traffic. The main streets in cities and suburban areas can have as many as four or even six lanes of traffic. **Freeways** or **expressways** often have more than six lanes in heavily-traveled urban areas. The roads and highways that connect our towns and cities vary from small, two-lane rural roads to large six-lane interstate highways.

An engineer planning a road has to consider how much traffic will use it and how fast that traffic will be going. Fast-moving traffic, especially heavy trucks, puts great stress on the road surface and foundations. Main roads are strengthened to take this stress.

Joining roads

If you see a new road being built, you may find work going on in a number of different places and wonder how it will all come together. Road junctions, bridges, and overpasses are all built at the same time. Structures such as these must fit together exactly. The planning and calculations may go on for years before construction begins.

Complicated junctions are built where highways meet to allow drivers to change roads. This junction in Great Britain is known as Spaghetti Junction.

Making a road

When a new road is to be built, earth-moving equipment is brought in to clear the route of trees and rocks. Rocks are sometimes blown up with explosives. Earth may have to be moved to make the route more level. Dips and hollows may have to be filled in. In other places, a level path may have to be cut through the side of a hill. When this has been done, the earth is **compacted,** or made solid, with a compacting machine.

A paving truck blacktops a road with an asphalt mixture. The surface must be smooth and firm, and allow water to flow off it.

Layers of a road

A paved road is usually made of different layers.

The **surface,** or top layer, is made of concrete or asphalt. Asphalt contains bitumen, a kind of tar.

Next is a **base** layer of a compacted material, including sand or stones, which provides drainage and support.

At the bottom, the **subgrade** is the natural soil or rock. The soil is compacted to make it solid.

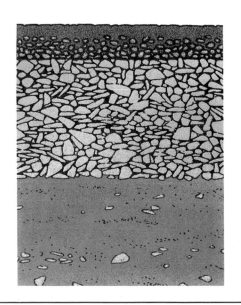

Find out more by looking at pages **50–51**

Under your feet

If you could see through the pavement under your feet, this is what you might see. There is a network of pipes, tunnels, and cables down there. They branch off to houses, offices, and stores all over the city. Water and gas flow through pipes, and telephone and electrical signals are carried through cables. These pipes and cables are buried out of sight underneath the roads.

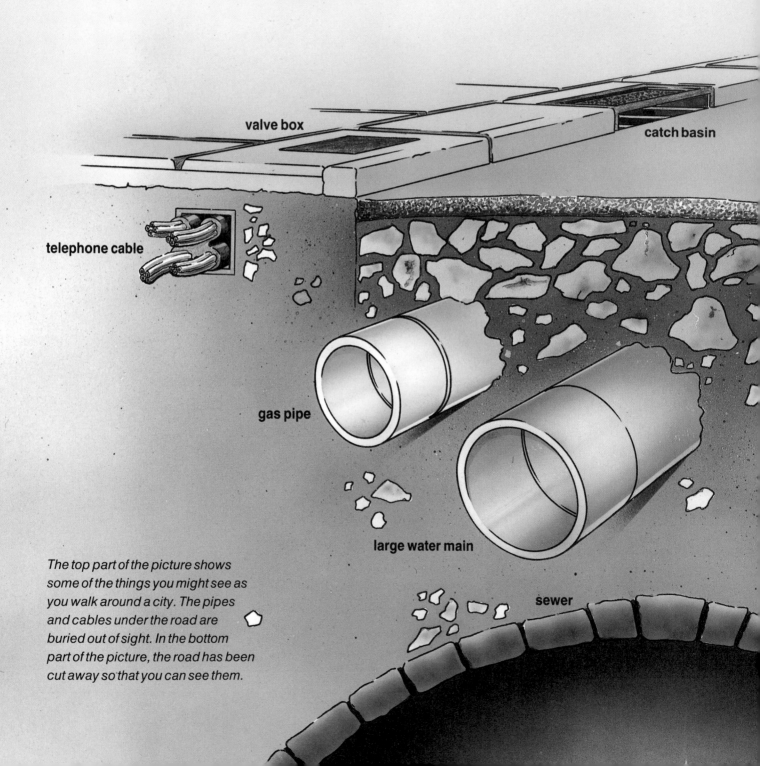

valve box

catch basin

telephone cable

gas pipe

large water main

sewer

The top part of the picture shows some of the things you might see as you walk around a city. The pipes and cables under the road are buried out of sight. In the bottom part of the picture, the road has been cut away so that you can see them.

Draining away

When you let the water out of your bathtub, it goes down the drain of your house into a larger drain, or **sewer.** The waste water from all the sinks, bathtubs, and toilets in the buildings in your street drains into the sewer. It flows to a sewage treatment plant where it is cleaned. Rain water also flows into the sewer. The surface of a road is slightly arched, or **cambered.** This allows rain water to flow away from the road surface into the gutters and down the catch basins, thus preventing the roads from becoming flooded.

fire hydrant

manhole

metal plate

electricity cable

small water main

gas pipe

Underground repairs

Maintenance workers need to inspect or repair underground pipes and cables. They reach them through special openings in the ground.

Valve boxes allow water companies to turn off the water supply for repairs.

Manholes enable sewer workers to climb down into sewers.

Metal plates in the pavement can be lifted up, so maintenance workers can reach telephone, TV and electricity cables, and gas pipes.

Keeping out moisture

Everyone wants to live in a place that is dry. No one wants to stay in a building that is damp.

Dampness can enter a building in three ways. Moisture can creep up from the ground and through the floor and walls. Second, rain or snow can come in through the roof.

Third, moisture is produced inside the building. Water vapor or steam is released when people heat liquids for cooking, and when people exhale.

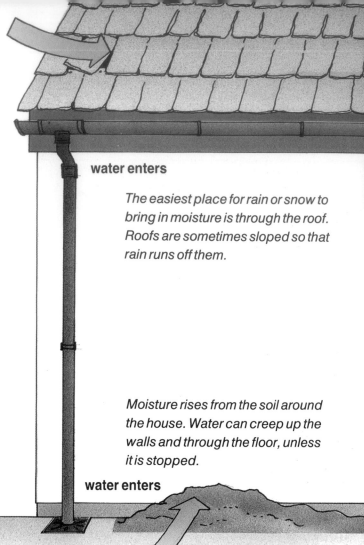

water enters

The easiest place for rain or snow to bring in moisture is through the roof. Roofs are sometimes sloped so that rain runs off them.

Moisture rises from the soil around the house. Water can creep up the walls and through the floor, unless it is stopped.

water enters

Rising moisture

Moisture can come up into a building from the ground. Try this experiment to see how water rises through sand.

You will need:

a glass tumbler full of dry sand or soil

water

a shallow dish

a cup with a pouring spout, such as a measuring cup

1. Put the dish upside down on top of the tumbler full of sand.

2. Now hold them tightly together and turn them upside down. Add about ½ inch (1.25 centimeters) of water to the dish.

Steam rises from hot water in the kitchen. The steam cools and leaves moisture everywhere.

Danger: Hot water can scald.

steam rises

Halting moisture

How can you stop the water from rising? Try another experiment.

You will need:

a plastic bag

a large tray

scissors

water

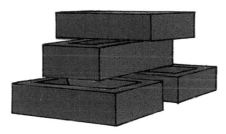

four dry bricks

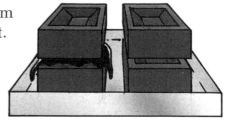

1. Put two bricks in the tray. Cut a piece of plastic the same size as a brick. Place it on top of one of the bricks. Put another brick on top of each brick, so you have two pairs.

2. Add 1 inch (2.5 centimeters) of water to the tray. Inspect the experiment after one day to see what has happened. Explain.

What is damp proofing?

The water level has gone down. Where has the water gone? Look at the bottom bricks in each pile and you will see that they are both damp. Feel the top brick in each pile. Is it also damp? Does it look dry? Water has risen up both bottom bricks—but the plastic stopped it from rising farther in one pair of bricks. Sheets made of thick plastic or other materials are built into walls and ground-level floors to keep moisture from rising into houses and other buildings.

3. Look at the sand through the glass every five minutes. What is happening? Why does some of the sand become darker?

Insulation

Most buildings are used as shelters. The people inside the buildings need to feel comfortable, whatever the temperature may be outside. So heat must be trapped inside or kept out. This is done by **insulation.**

Keeping heat in

On a cold day, warm air inside a building escapes to the cold air outside. We can reduce the amount of heat lost by insulating the places where heat is most likely to escape, such as the roof and the windows. Anything that traps air and prevents the movement of heat is a good **insulator.** A thick layer of fiberglass or mineral wool fiber in the roof space is a good insulator. Another is liquid plastic foam sprayed into the space between the outer and inner walls. Double glazing consists of two sheets of glass with a narrow air gap between them. It helps to cut the loss of heat through windows. It also helps insulate the building against noise.

Keeping heat out

The same kinds of insulation help to keep the outside heat out. Large modern buildings and many small buildings also have ventilation systems that pump cool, fresh air in and take warm, stale air away.

Birds fluff out their feathers in cold weather. This traps a layer of air next to their skin. The air is warmed by the birds' body heat and keeps them warm.

Testing insulating materials

What sort of materials provide the best insulation? You can try this experiment to find out.

You will need:

Some warm water cool enough to put your hand in

six rubber bands

a newspaper

absorbent cotton

a cloth

four glass jars

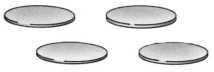

four cardboard lids to cover the jars

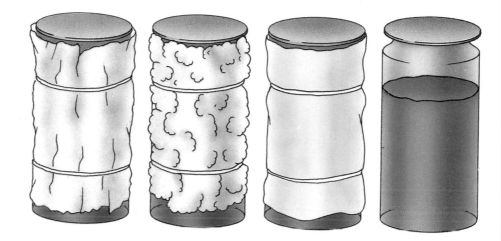

1. Stand the jars in a row on the table several inches apart. Wrap the first jar with a layer of newspaper. Wrap the second jar with a layer of loose cotton and the third with a layer of cloth. Attach the layers of insulation with two rubber bands each.

2. Leave the fourth jar unwrapped.

3. Fill each jar with warm water and cover with the lids.

4. Every ten minutes, lift each lid and feel how warm the water is in each jar. If you have a thermometer at home, you could use it to measure the temperature of the water.

5. Which jar stays warm the longest? Which material works best as an insulator? Use your notebook to record your findings.

Structures in the future

Since the year 1900, the world's population has tripled. Each year, there are about 90 million more people in need of space. No wonder people worry about conservation and whether we can continue to feed and care for so many.

Engineers and architects may dream of "cities of the future," but will these help? Could you live in a great city built entirely under the ground? Could you live in a science fiction city floating in space? Of course, there are huge areas of the earth where nobody lives. Very few people live at the North and South poles, or in the deserts and the mountains. The climate is too harsh for people to live comfortably in these places.

New structures

One day, scientists may develop a way in which people can live in unusual places. Perhaps people would need to live in a vast, sealed building where the temperature can be controlled. Here, rain would fall at the touch of a button. Crops would grow and animals would be raised. The scientists would even be able to create oceans, lakes, and forests.

Sealed cities could be used in deserts or in very cold places. They could even be built on other planets, far out in space.

Scientists have already designed a sealed city, called Biosphere II. People are living in it on a desert in Arizona. Can you imagine a city like Biosphere where people live and farm in an environment which is completely controlled?

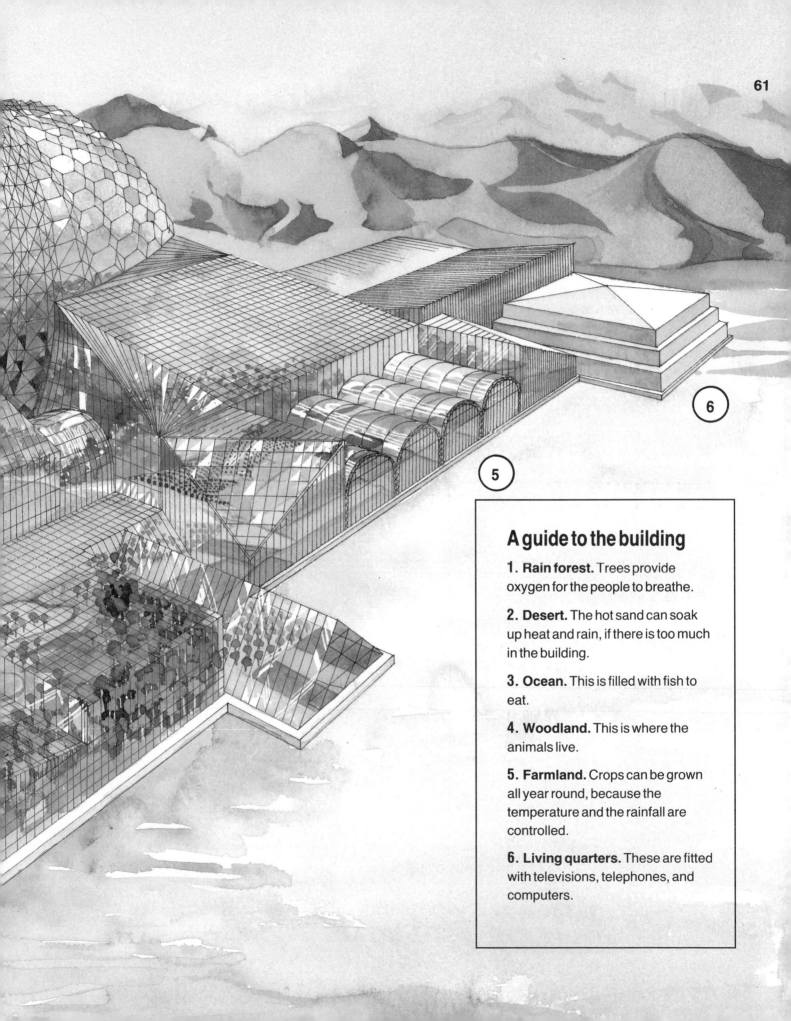

A guide to the building

1. Rain forest. Trees provide oxygen for the people to breathe.

2. Desert. The hot sand can soak up heat and rain, if there is too much in the building.

3. Ocean. This is filled with fish to eat.

4. Woodland. This is where the animals live.

5. Farmland. Crops can be grown all year round, because the temperature and the rainfall are controlled.

6. Living quarters. These are fitted with televisions, telephones, and computers.

MACHINES

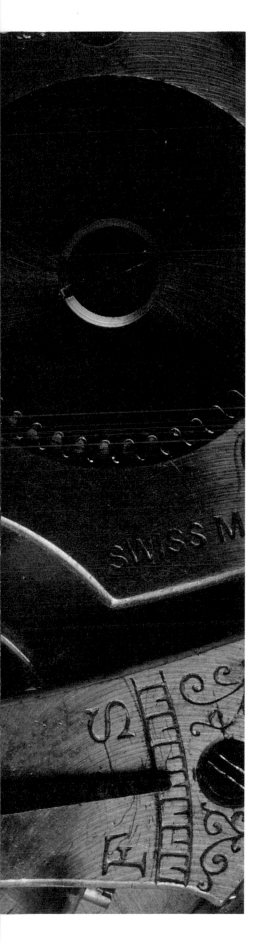

Making life easier

Can you imagine what our lives would be like without machines? Look around you at all the machines used every day. There are bicycles, cars, trains, airplanes, and cranes. At home, we have sewing machines, pianos, and clocks. Machines are everywhere—at home, at work, on the roads, at sea, in the air, and even in space.

These machines make our lives easier. They help us with our work. A car moves us from place to place. A sewing machine stitches through cloth. A mechanical clock helps us to measure time.

Simple machines

Most machines we use today are made up of many moving parts. Each part is a simple machine. Some machines are so simple that they don't appear to be machines at all. Levers, wedges, inclined planes, screws, wheels and axles, and pulleys are all simple machines. Most machines are made up of one or more of these six simple machines.

Machines at work

But machines cannot work on their own. We have to put some energy into them. A car needs gasoline to burn as fuel. A sewing machine is driven by an electric motor. The energy for a mechanical clock comes from a spring or a weight. Fuel, electricity, a wound-up spring, or a falling weight all supply energy to machines. Machines need energy to work.

Inside a mechanical clock, there are many moving parts, called gears. Gears turn the hands of the clock to show us the time of day.

Perpetual motion

For hundreds of years, people have been trying to build a
perpetual motion machine — that is, a machine that, once set
in motion, will drive itself forever. There have been many
attempts at such an invention, but none of them has ever
worked.

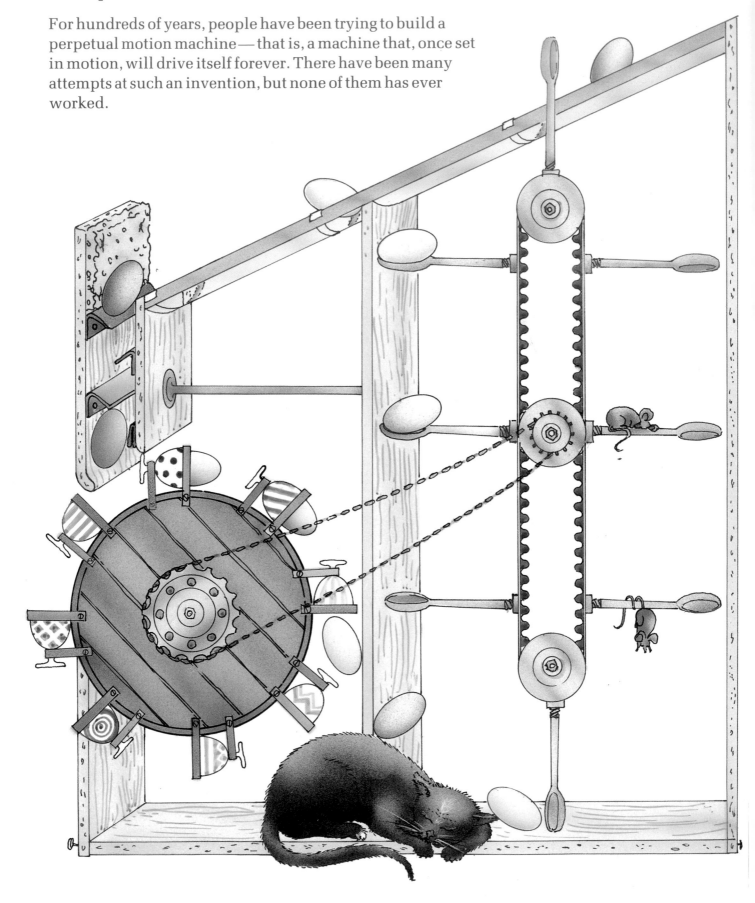

This machine looks as though it is driven by the weight of falling eggs. But it cannot work. Can you explain why?

Starting up the machine

Machines need energy to make them work. This energy can come from us. Our pedal power drives a bicycle. Energy can also come from electricity or from burning fuels.

But what happens to the energy we put into the machine? Inside the machine, the energy turns the moving parts. As they turn, the parts rub together and become hot. This rubbing together is called **friction.** Some of the energy has turned into heat. So not all the energy is passed on as movement through the machine. But the energy that is passed on does useful work.

A simple machine, like a lever, works well. The work it does is almost equal to the energy put into it. But a car engine uses only about a quarter of the energy it receives from burning gasoline. Most of the energy is lost as heat. One reason that perpetual motion machines cannot work is that they lose energy through friction. All machines need a steady supply of energy to keep them working.

Effort and work

Imagine you are cycling from the bottom of a steep hill to the top. There are two routes that you can take. The first route goes straight up the side of the hill. The second route winds around and around the hill. The first route is shorter but will take a lot of effort. The second route is longer but will need less effort. Whichever route you take, you will do the same amount of **work.** Work measures the amount of effort, or **force,** you use over a **distance.** Scientists use a short way of expressing this relationship: **w**ork = **f**orce x **d**istance.

Work and power

Suppose you and your friend are racing each other to the top of the hill, both taking the same route. You take 10 minutes to reach the top. Your friend arrives 5 minutes later. Both of you have done the same amount of work, but you have worked faster. You have used more power to take you to the top of the hill more quickly. **Power** is the amount of work you can do during a length of time. The more powerful a machine is, the faster it can work. Again, scientists have a short way of stating this: **p**ower = **f**orce x **d**istance/**t**ime.

These football players are running and pushing against each other. Running and pushing are forces that cause changes in motion.

Forces in action

What do you think happens if you place a ball on a flat surface? It stays still. If you push it, the ball starts to move in a straight line. If you give it another push, you can make it go in another direction. Try pushing a heavy ball and a light ball — which is easier to start moving?

Pushing and pulling usually set things in motion. This is because pushing and pulling are **forces.** A force always makes objects move or changes their direction. Machines work on the same principle. The machine's engine changes energy into a force that sets the machine in motion. The machine passes on these forces from one part of the machine to another, constantly changing direction.

Find out more by looking at pages **84–85**

Resisting change

Have you ever stood on a bus or a train when it has suddenly come to a halt? Usually, you almost fall over! This is because, although the vehicle has stopped, your body is still traveling forward. Your body is resisting the change from moving forward to standing still. This resistance to change is called **inertia.** When the bus starts moving again, you will feel yourself being pulled backward. This time, your body is resisting the change from standing still to moving forward. Your body eventually overcomes the inertia as the bus moves along. Machine engines also must overcome inertia.

There are other forces acting on machines, too. The force that pulls objects towards the earth is called **gravity.** If you hold a ball in the air and let go, it will fall to the ground. The force of gravity has pulled it downward. Some machines, like the grandfather clock, can use this force of the pull of gravity to help them work.

When a bus moves suddenly, the passengers are jolted. This is caused by inertia.

Friction

Place an ice cube, a block of wood, a matchbox, and an eraser on a table. Give each one a little push. What happens? The ice cube will move easily, but the eraser will be difficult to push. There is a force that stops it from moving. This force is called **friction.** Friction happens when two surfaces rub together.

Rub two sheets of smooth paper together, then rub two pieces of rough sandpaper. There is much less friction between smooth surfaces than between rough surfaces.

Try pushing a light book across the table. Now push a heavy book. There is more friction between the heavy book and the table than between the light book and the table. Gravity is also pulling on the books, as it does on all matter.

Machines have many moving parts which rub together. Power is wasted because of friction between the parts. Friction also wears down the engine parts and eventually prevents them from working properly.

But without friction, vehicles could not move. Their wheels would simply spin around. This happens when wheels try to move on ice. Ice has a smooth surface which causes little friction. The wheels need friction to grip the road and move forwards.

Before you try pushing the block of wood and the matchbox, which do you think will produce the most friction? Ask yourself the same question in another way.

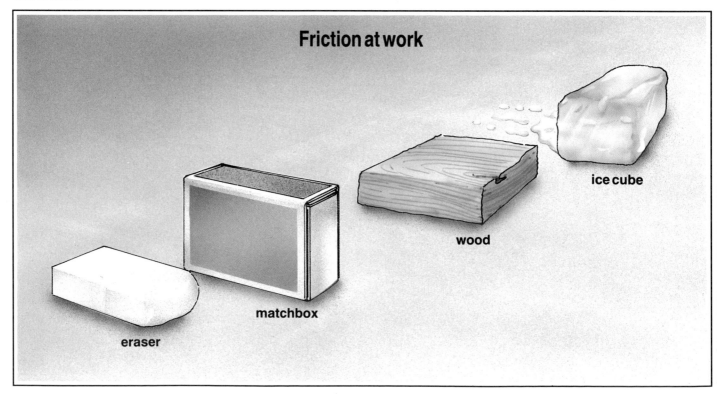

Friction at work

ice cube

wood

matchbox

eraser

The heat of friction

If you have a bicycle, try riding and then braking very hard. Now feel the brakes on your bike. You will find that they are hot. Friction causes heat. This heat is the energy of movement that the bike had when it was moving and which has now changed into the energy of heat. Without friction, vehicles would not be able to stop quickly.

Reducing friction

There are two main ways of reducing friction in machines. One is to keep them well oiled, or **lubricated.** There is less friction between the smooth coat of oil and the machine parts.

The other way of reducing friction is to use **ball-bearings.** The moving parts are kept apart with balls which can roll about.

Rolling marbles

Try this activity to show how ball-bearings help reduce friction.

You will need:

two cans that fit together, one on top of the other (cans should be full, not empty)

marbles

1. Place one can on top of the other. Try to spin the top one around.

2. Now put a handful of marbles between the top can and the bottom can. Does the top can spin now? Explain.

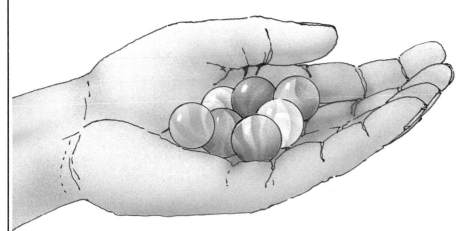

What is a lever?

A spoon is such a simple object that it hardly seems like a machine at all. But it can be one. It can turn the force and weight of your hand into movement to lift the lid off a tin can. The spoon is a type of simple machine called a **lever.** All levers have an arm that can rock, or pivot, around a support called a **fulcrum.** The fulcrum can be anywhere along the length of the arm. Levers are used to make work easier.

Spoon power

Try taking the lid off a can using a coin. Fit one edge of the coin under the rim of the lid and push down on the opposite edge of the coin. The edge of the can acts as a fulcrum. It can be quite difficult if the lid is fitted tightly. Now try using the handle of a teaspoon, pressing down on the bowl of the spoon. You will probably find it easier to take the lid off. If you use a spoon with a longer handle, it is even easier.

As you push the bowl of the spoon down, the force of your effort acts upon the other end of the spoon and pushes it up. The bowl of the spoon moves down through a longer distance than the handle moves up. So the force is greater on the handle end. Force is equal to effort times distance.

A spoon acts as a lever to take the lid off a can. The fulcrum is the edge of the can. The load is the lid. And the effort is supplied by the hand.

Types of levers

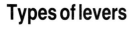

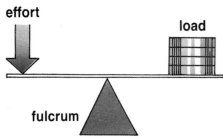

A lever like the spoon is called a **first-class lever.** So too is a seesaw. The fulcrum of a first-class lever is between the effort and the load.

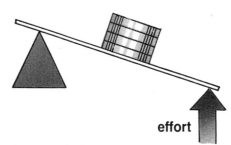

A **second-class lever** has the fulcrum at one end. An effort at the other end lifts a load between the fulcrum and the effort. A wheelbarrow is an example.

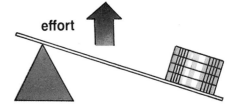

A **third-class lever** also has the fulcrum at one end. But it has the load at the other end. The effort is applied between the fulcrum and the load. Your arm is an example of this kind of lever.

You will need:

a pencil

a wooden ruler

some heavy coins

1. Place the pencil on a flat table—place the ruler across the pencil so that both ends of the ruler balance without touching the table.

2. Now place a coin on one end. This is your load. The other end of the ruler will tip up.

3. Place another coin on the other end so that both balance again. This second coin acts as your effort.

4. If you add three more coins to one end, the other end of the ruler will tip up once more.

5. But if you move the pencil toward the heavy end of the ruler, you should be able to balance the ruler with only one coin on the other end.

Balance your money

This activity will show you how to lift four heavy coins using the same effort as it takes to lift one heavy coin.

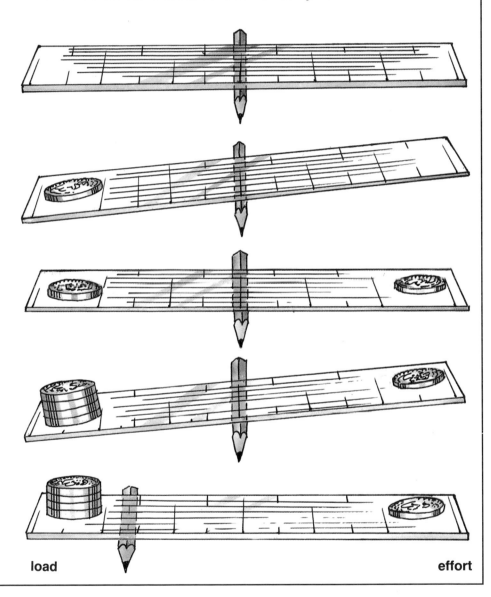

load   effort

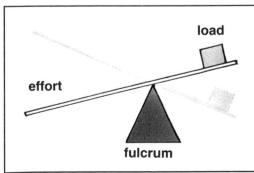

Mechanical advantage

Levers give us a **mechanical advantage.** Mechanical advantage is the extra force we gain from using simple machines. In this example, the fulcrum is placed two-thirds of the way along the lever.

So the force at the lifting end, the load force, will be twice as great as the force at the handle end, the effort force. This lever gives us a mechanical advantage of two. Mechanical advantage is a mathematical relationship.

A machine for war

Some of the first machines were invented for war. Huge machines, called **catapults**, were built to hurl rocks at castles and fortresses.

One type of catapult was built of huge beams of wood. One end of a large wooden lever was bound by ropes to another piece of wood called a **crossbeam.** The crossbeam had rope coiled tightly around it. The other end of the lever had a large bowl, like a spoon, and was tied down. A large boulder was placed in the bowl of the lever. Using heavy beams, the soldiers turned the crossbeam around, twisting the rope tighter and tighter, like a spring. Then the rope holding down the bowl of the lever was released. The lever swung up, hurling the boulder into the air.

The catapult could hurl huge stones against or over the high walls of a city or castle.

You will need:

two small nails

two large nails

two wide rubber bands

a plastic spoon

paper

a block of wood about 4 in (10 cm) across and 9 in (22.5 cm) long

a hammer

Make a catapult

You can make a simple catapult machine using some rubber bands and a plastic spoon as a lever.

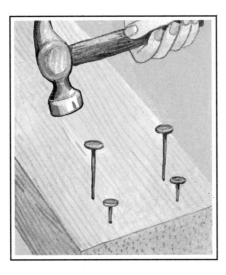

1. Ask an adult to hammer four nails into the block of wood. The two large nails should be fixed about 1 inch (2.5 centimeters) behind the small nails.

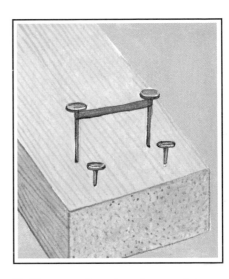

2. Place a rubber band around the two large nails. Twist another band and place it over the small nails.

3. Insert the handle of the spoon under the first rubber band and through the twisted-up rubber band. Now hold down the bowl of the spoon.

4. Place a small piece of crumpled paper in the bowl of the spoon. Check that no one is in your line of fire before letting go of the spoon.

Levers and strings—grand piano

If you look around you, you can find machines to carry out almost any kind of work. You can probably also find some machines which are made just for fun.

The **grand piano** is a machine for making music. It uses levers and strings to produce sounds. The sounds come from thin wires that have been stretched in a frame. As the player pushes a key on the piano keyboard, a series of levers connected together moves a hammer to strike the wire strings.

The strings are arranged in a special way so that the sounds, or notes, gradually get higher as the keys are pressed from left to right. The longer, thicker strings at the left of the frame produce the lower notes. As the strings become shorter and thinner across the frame, the notes produced become higher. The piano body acts as an amplifier, making the sound from the moving, or vibrating, strings louder.

keyboard

pedals

The keyboard contains 88 keys. Fifty-two of these are white, and 36 are black. Each key gives a different sound, or note. The keys on the right-hand side of the keyboard give higher notes than the keys on the left-hand side of the keyboard.

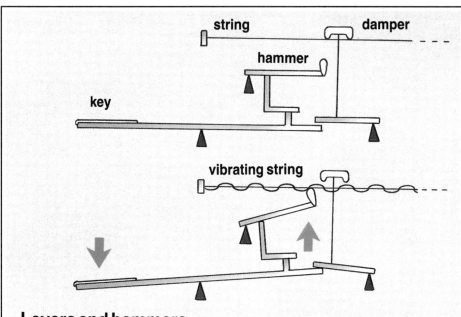

string   damper

hammer

key

vibrating string

Levers and hammers

The parts of a piano that make the notes sound are called the **action.** This is how the action works. When the pianist presses a key on the **keyboard,** a system of levers moves a hammer.

The **hammer** is made of wood and covered with a special kind of felt. The hammer strikes a **string,** which vibrates and makes a sound. When the pianist releases the key, a **damper** presses against the string to stop the sound.

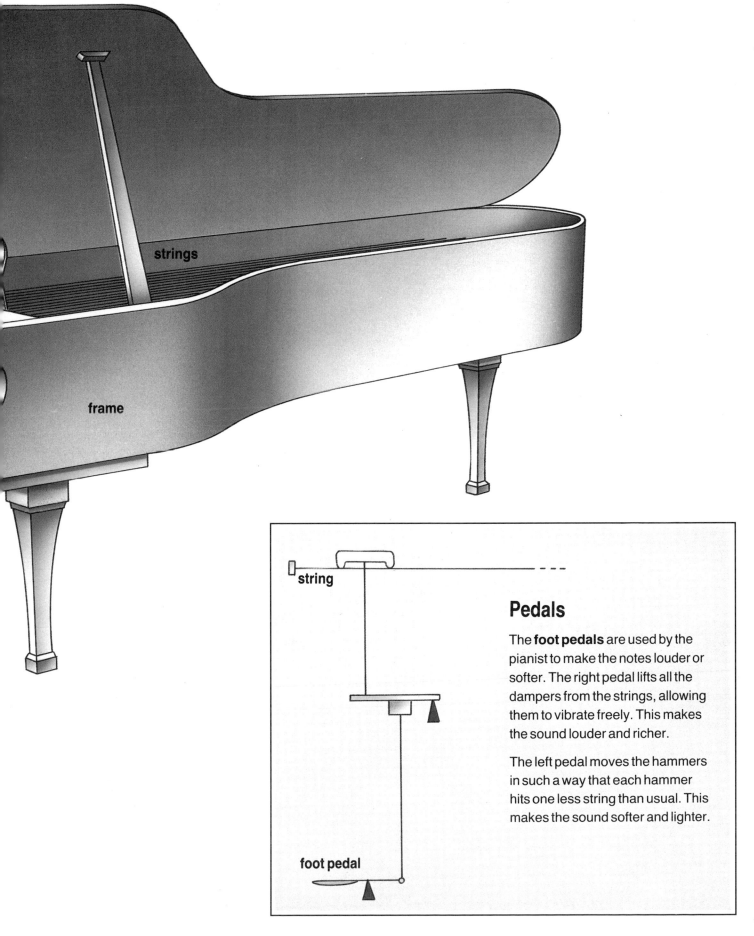

strings

frame

string

foot pedal

Pedals

The **foot pedals** are used by the pianist to make the notes louder or softer. The right pedal lifts all the dampers from the strings, allowing them to vibrate freely. This makes the sound louder and richer.

The left pedal moves the hammers in such a way that each hammer hits one less string than usual. This makes the sound softer and lighter.

Inclined planes and wedges

If you are pushing a heavy wheelbarrow and you come to a step, how do you get up the step? You can't lift the wheelbarrow because it is too heavy. Find a plank and rest one end on the top of the step. Now you can push the wheelbarrow up the sloping plank more easily.

The slope, in this case a plank, is a simple machine called an **inclined plane.** Instead of using a lot of effort over a short distance to lift the wheelbarrow over the step, you use a smaller effort over a larger distance—up the sloping plank.

Cars need inclined planes to drive to the top of a mountain. An ordinary car is not powerful enough to climb up a very steep slope. So roads wind their way up the slopes. They snake from side to side as they climb the mountainside gradually.

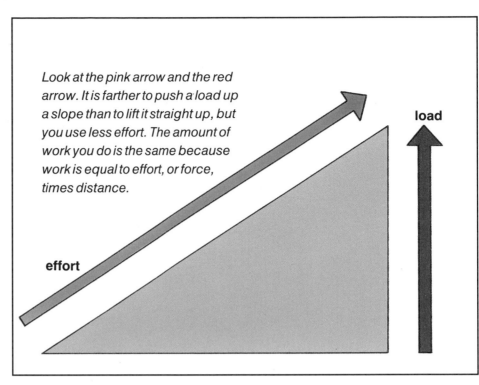

Look at the pink arrow and the red arrow. It is farther to push a load up a slope than to lift it straight up, but you use less effort. The amount of work you do is the same because work is equal to effort, or force, times distance.

This winding mountain road is an inclined plane. By taking a longer, but less steep route, a car can easily reach the top of the mountain.

Working wedges

When you put two inclined planes together, back to back, you make a **wedge.** This is also a simple machine. A wedge changes the direction of a force and increases it.

An axe is a wedge used as a cutting machine. The long movement of the axe downwards creates a strong, sideways force that splits open the wood. A blunt axe has a wide wedge. This has a small splitting force. A sharp axe has a narrow wedge. This has a greater splitting force.

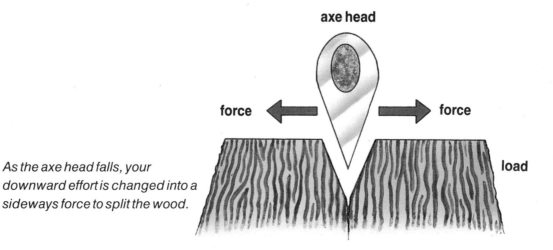

As the axe head falls, your downward effort is changed into a sideways force to split the wood.

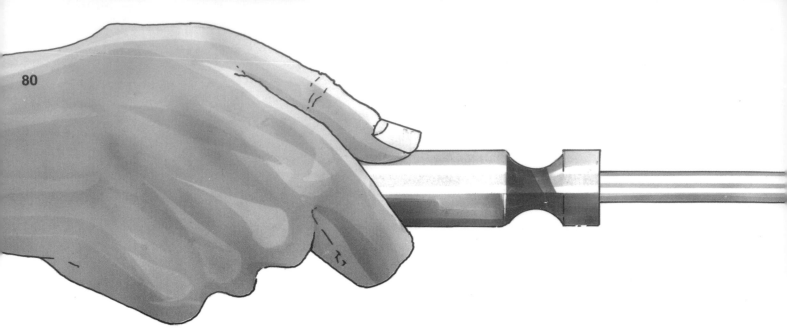

Screws are machines

We don't usually think of **screws** as machines. We use them to hold things together. But a screw is a simple machine. It has a ridge, called a **thread,** cut around it in the form of a spiral. It is a special kind of inclined plane that twists and turns.

The screw is much better at increasing forces than other simple machines. To turn a screw, you apply a turning force to the head of the screw. A point on the spiral edge of the screw travels quite a long way when you turn the head of the screw around once. This means you are applying your force over quite a long distance to make the screw move forward a very small distance. This gives the screw a huge mechanical advantage. It can increase the force you put into it very many times.

Nuts and bolts

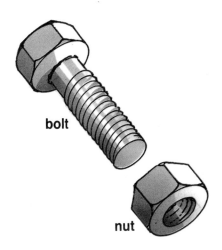

There are several kinds of screws. Some fasten directly into wood or other material. This type of screw is wide at the head and becomes narrower towards the tip. It has quite a coarse or wide thread. Another kind of screw is used to fasten two or more parts together. This screw is shaped like a cylinder and usually has a finer, narrower thread. It is often called a **bolt.** It fits into a **nut,** which also has a thread. The thread of the bolt screws into the thread on the nut. The head of the bolt and the nut are sometimes hexagonal—they have six sides. They are tightened with a wrench. The wrench acts like a lever to apply a strong force to the nut.

bolt

nut

Jacking it up

Have you ever tried lifting a car? It sounds impossible, but motorists need to lift their cars to change a tire. To do this they use a car **jack,** also called a **jackscrew.** Most jacks have a screw that can turn inside a nut. By cranking the handle of the jack, you turn a screw that raises an arm that lifts up the car. The handle applies your effort over a long distance. Then the screw exerts a huge force on the arm as it moves up just a little way. Using a simple car jack, a driver can easily lift a vehicle weighing a ton or more.

You will need:

several screws and bolts of different sizes

colored chalk

a sheet of white paper

ruler with centimeter markings

What's the advantage?

You can work out how much a screw increases a force. This is the screw's mechanical advantage.

1. Try a wood screw first. Measure the distance around the edge of the screw's head. To do this, rub colored chalk all around the edge of the screw's head. Then roll the head on the paper for one complete revolution. Measure the chalk line drawn.

2. Now measure the distance between the threads by measuring from one thread down to the next.

3. If you divide the first number by the second number, you will find the mechanical advantage.

4. Repeat the experiment for different sizes of screws and bolts. You should find that some bolts can increase a force 35 or 40 times.

The distance between two peaks of the thread is called the **pitch.** When a screw turns around once, it moves forward an amount equal to the pitch.

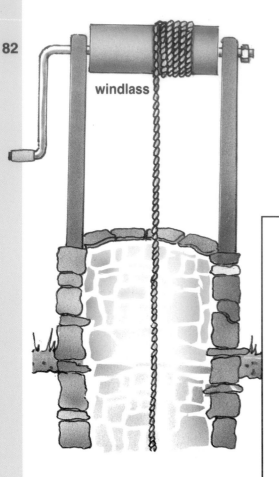

windlass

Wheels and axles

There are many machines that use wheels of some sort, inside or out. Some machines, such as cars and trains, move along on wheels. Other machines, such as sewing machines, have wheels that turn other parts. If you looked inside an old-fashioned clock, you would find all sorts of wheels of many different sizes.

This windlass, or winch, raises water from a well. A rope is tied to the bucket and wound around a roller, or axle. At one end of the axle is a handle. When you turn the handle once, in a large circle, the axle turns once, in a small circle. The rope and bucket move up a short distance.

Using wheels and axles

The wheels on a vehicle are attached to a long rod called an **axle.** A wheel and axle is a simple machine. Try making a tractor with wheels and axles. What advantage does a tractor give its user?

You will need:

some cardboard

two pencils with round sides

a matchbox

scissors

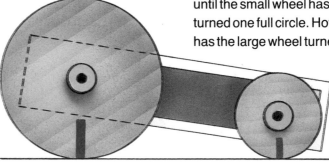

1. Push the pencils through opposite sides of the matchbox near the bottom at each end.

2. Cut two large circles 2 in (5 cm) in diameter and two small circles 1 in (2.5 cm) in diameter from the cardboard.

3. Make a mark on the edge of each wheel. Push the wheels onto the pencils.

4. Make sure the marks on the front wheel and back wheel are pointing toward the ground. Now move the tractor forward until the small wheel has turned one full circle. How far has the large wheel turned?

Gears

Inside machines, wheels often have notches, or **cogs,** cut around the edge. Wheels like this are called **gears.** Each gear fits with another to pass on a desired motion of the machine. Gears are also useful for changing the direction and speed of movement.

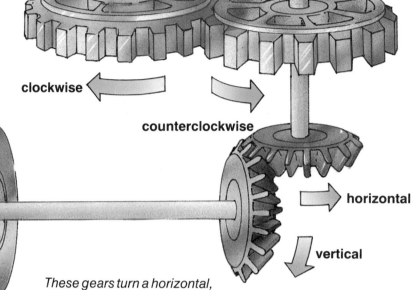

These gears turn a clockwise movement into a counterclockwise movement.

clockwise

counterclockwise

These gears turn a slow movement into a fast movement.

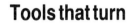

slow

fast

horizontal

vertical

These gears turn a horizontal, circular movement into a vertical, circular movement.

Tools that turn

A number of tools use the idea of the wheel and axle, but have no wheels at all! The handle of a screwdriver turns a shaft.

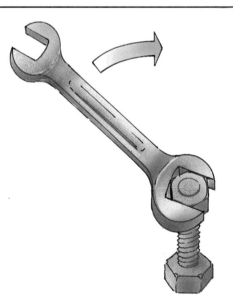

A wrench turns in a wide circle to move the bolt inside the nut.

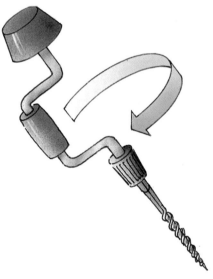

A carpenter's brace and bit has a bent handle, so it turns in a large circle. It makes the drill bit turn in a small circle with greater force.

Cogs, gears, and wheels

One of the most important machines is used to measure time. The very first clocks were powered by water. Today, many clocks and watches are electronic. But there are still many mechanical clocks. This type of clock gave its name to the **clockwork** mechanism.

There are two types of mechanical clocks. Large mechanical clocks, like the pendulum clock, are often driven by a weight. Smaller mechanical clocks and watches are often driven by small springs called mainsprings.

The pendulum clock

Inside the **pendulum clock,** also known as a **weight-driven clock,** there is a heavy weight that hangs from a cord or a chain. The cord is attached to a drum, which is connected to a series of gears. Each of these gears has a different number of cogs, the "teeth" along the edge, and moves at a different, but steady speed. The gears move the hands of the clock. When the clock is wound, the cord wraps around the drum, pulling the weight up. When the weight begins to fall, the cord unwinds and turns the drum. This sets the gears moving, each one at its own set speed, and these turn the hands of the clock.

verge

weight

pendulum

This cutaway picture of a pendulum clock shows the gears, pendulum, and weight inside.

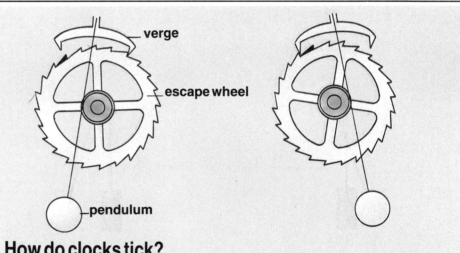

verge

escape wheel

pendulum

How do clocks tick?

The part of the clock that makes the ticking sound is called the **escapement.** As the pendulum swings, the verge rocks backwards and forwards. As it rocks, it catches the cogs of the escape wheel, alternately stopping it and then releasing it to turn slightly.

Spring-driven clocks

A **spring-driven clock** or watch has a winding device. When this device is turned, a mainspring inside winds tighter. Then, as the spring slowly unwinds, the gears start to move around. The movement is controlled by an escapement, which regulates the speed of the movement of the hands.

Clockwork toys

It is not only clocks and watches that are driven by clockwork mechanisms. Many toys are powered by springs. There is often a key in the side of the toy. This is wound to tighten a spring inside the toy. Clockwork toys move smoothly, slowing down as the spring unwinds.

As the spring in this robot unwinds, the large gear wheel turns the rod. At each end of the rod, an egg-shaped disk joins the rod to the robot's legs. When the rod turns, the disks lift each leg and move them forwards, one at a time, in a circular movement.

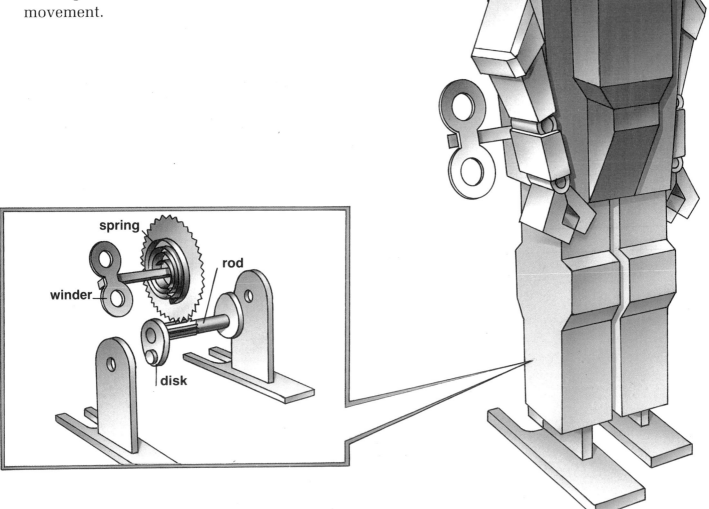

On two wheels

The bicycle is the cheapest form of mechanical transport because it does not use an expensive fuel. It works on muscle power. You are the engine! The bicycle is made up of many small machines, which work together to make it easy and comfortable to ride. All these parts are held together by the bicycle frame, which is usually metal.

Suspension

The bicycle saddle is fitted with springs. They help cushion the rider over bumpy roads. The springs form part of the **suspension.** The tires also act like springs to make the ride more comfortable. They are made of rubber and have inner tubes filled with air. They are called **pneumatic,** or air-filled, tires.

Transmission

The bicycle chain acts as the **transmission.** It carries the movement of the pedals to the back wheel. Cogs in the chainwheel fit into slots in the chain. The chain then passes around a smaller rear wheel, called a sprocket. This is fixed to the center, or hub, of the back wheel. The chainwheel and the sprocket form part of the **gears** of the bike. Most bikes have a number of sprockets of different sizes. These turn the back wheel at different speeds, to suit the steepness of the road.

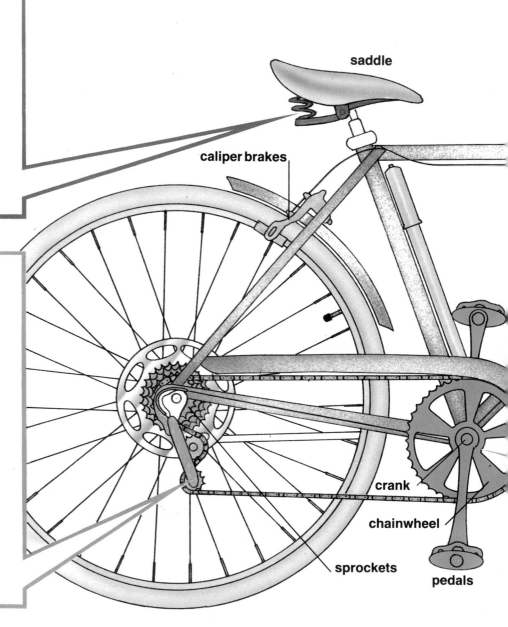

saddle

caliper brakes

crank

chainwheel

sprockets

pedals

Steering

The handle bars are attached to the front fork, which holds the front wheel. As you pull the left or right handle bar towards you, the fork points the front of the wheel in the direction you want to go.

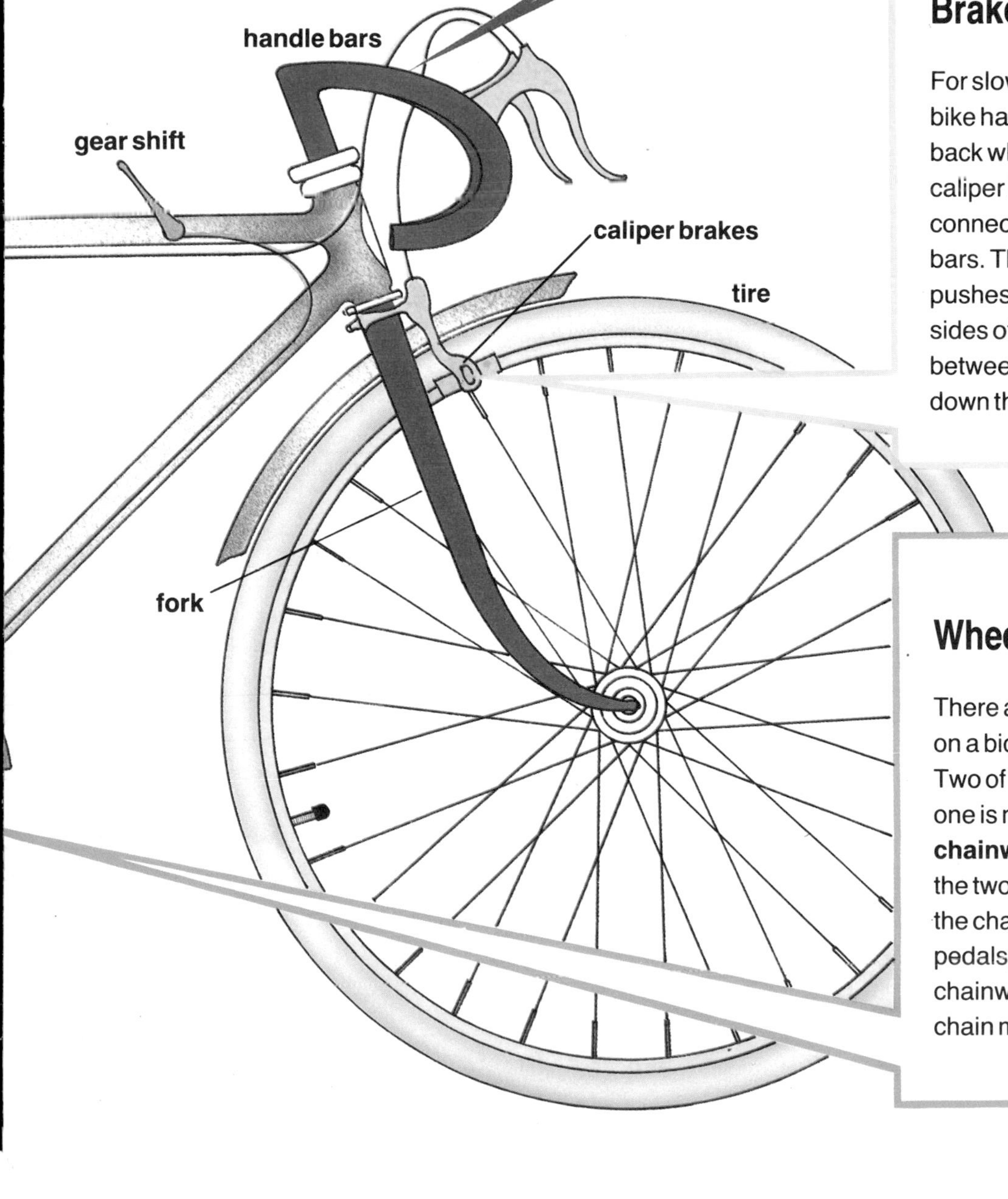

handle bars

gear shift

caliper brakes

tire

fork

Brakes

For slowing down and stopping, the bike has **brakes** on the front and back wheels. Most bikes have caliper brakes. These are connected to levers on the handle bars. The levers pull a cable, which pushes in brake pads to grip the sides of the wheel rim. **Friction** between the pads and the rim slows down the wheel.

Wheels and axles

There are three wheels and axles on a bicycle. Can you find them? Two of them are obvious. The third one is made up of the **crank** and the **chainwheel.** The crank connects the two pedals through the center of the chainwheel. As you turn the pedals, the axle turns the chainwheel, which then makes the chain move around.

Pulleys — simple and complex

A **pulley** is a simple machine made up of wheels. A pulley wheel turns on an axle. There is a groove around the rim of the pulley wheel that holds a rope.

The simplest pulley system has one pulley wheel and a rope. Pulleys are used to lift heavy loads like the sails on a boat. The pulley is fixed to a beam above the load. The rope is tied at one end to the load and then goes up and over the pulley, the other end being free. You lift the load by pulling on the free end of the rope.

A rope and pulley do not increase the pull, or lifting force, that you apply to the rope. But they change the direction of your pull. Pulling down on something is much easier than lifting it up. This makes it easier for you to lift the load.

These cranes use pulleys to lift heavy building materials.

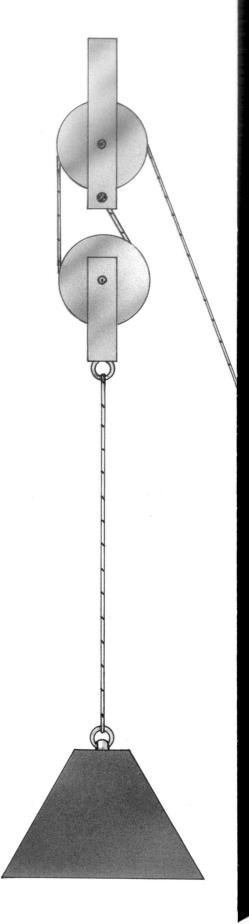

A pulley experiment

You can make a simple pulley wheel from a thread spool.

You will need:

stiff wire

string

a cup

a thread spool

1. Thread your wire through the thread spool and fix it in a high position, as shown.

2. Run a long piece of string around the thread spool and tie one end around a cup handle.

3. Your pulley and rope are now ready to lift a load.

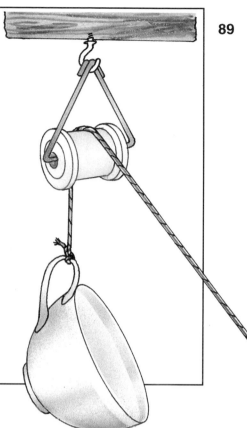

Block and tackle

You can increase your lifting force if you use two pulleys. One is fixed to an overhead beam as before. The other is fixed to the load. The rope is fixed to the beam, too. Then it goes under the load pulley and over the fixed pulley. You pull on the free end.

For every inch (2.5 centimeters) you pull the rope downward, the load moves up only ½ inch (1.25 centimeters). In other words, there is a mechanical advantage of two. So this system has doubled your lifting force.

A system with more than one pulley is known as a **block and tackle.** The pulleys are the blocks, and the rope is the tackle. By increasing the number of pulleys in a block and tackle, you can increase the lifting force even more. Using six pulleys, for example, will increase the lifting force six times. But the load will move up only one-sixth of the distance that the rope is pulled.

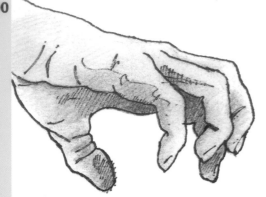

Driving machines with energy

Energy is all around us. There is energy in the wind when it blows, and in water when it flows. There is energy stored in fuels such as coal and gas. This energy is released when we burn them. There is energy in the electricity that flows along wires. There is energy, too, in the steam that spurts out of a boiling kettle. Machines can harness this energy and put it to work.

Steam engines, steam turbines, windmills, waterwheels, and gasoline engines turn this energy into a more useful form of energy—**mechanical energy.**

These machines are engines. Engines turn energy into mechanical work to drive other machines. For example, water turbines drive generators to make electricity, gasoline engines drive cars, and steam turbines drive ships.

Energy from steam

When we burn fuels, we release energy as heat. Heat energy can be transferred to water to make it boil. This is what happens inside a kettle. As the water boils, it turns into steam and takes up more space. The steam trapped inside the kettle presses against the kettle lid. The steam has **potential energy.** This is how a steam engine works. Steam builds up inside a huge boiler and pushes against the moving parts of the engine. These are the pistons. The potential energy of the steam has turned into mechanical energy.

Clouds of condensed steam can also escape through the kettle spout. Now the steam has **kinetic energy.** It could be used to drive a turbine. In a steam turbine, jets of steam blow against particular moving parts of the machine. The kinetic energy of the steam has turned into mechanical energy.

At rest and in motion

Hold a ball in your hand. Do you think it has any energy? Well, it has. It has stored energy, or **potential energy.** It gained this energy when you lifted it up. Now let go of the ball. What happens? The ball falls. It has the energy of motion—**kinetic energy.** The energy that was stored in the ball has been released. The potential energy has changed into kinetic energy.

When the steam engine was developed, more than 250 years ago, many new, steam-powered machines were built.

steamboat

steam engine

pumping station

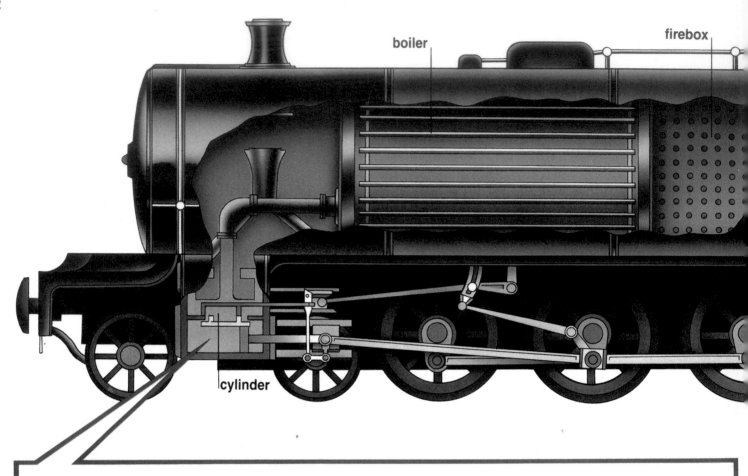

boiler

firebox

cylinder

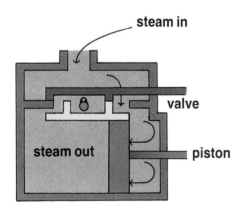

steam in

steam out

valve

piston

1. Steam from the boiler is fed into a cylinder. The steam pushes a piston inside the cylinder.

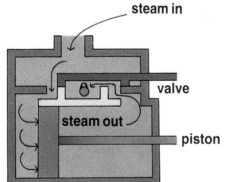

steam in

steam out

valve

piston

2. As the piston moves, a valve opens. The steam behind the piston escapes through the valve and out of the chimney.

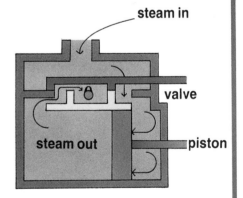

steam in

steam out

valve

piston

3. The piston and valve move backwards and forwards. The piston movement turns a wheel which drives the locomotive along.

Many steam engines have been replaced by internal combustion engines like the gas engine. But steam locomotives are still used to haul trains like this one at Mahesana Junction, India.

Getting up steam

Until about 100 years ago, most of the engines found in factories, ships, and railway locomotives were **steam engines.** Some of the most successful steam engines were the locomotives that hauled trains on the railways. Their powerful pistons drove wheels as tall as a human being. The largest of all locomotives were the American "Big Boys," which weighed over 550 short tons (500 metric tons) and had the power of 6,000 horses!

Steam engines are called **external combustion engines.** This means that their fuel is burned outside the engine cylinders. The engines are fueled by burning coal, wood, or oil in a firebox. The firebox heats water in the boiler until the water turns to steam. Exhaust gases from the firebox escape through a chimney. The steam is fed into a cylinder, where it drives a piston. This, in turn, drives the wheels that move the locomotive.

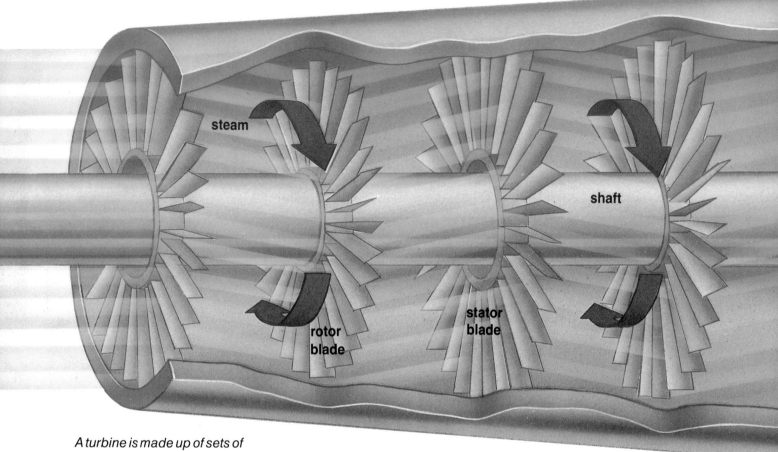

A turbine is made up of sets of curved rotor blades attached to a shaft. In a steam turbine, fixed blades, also called stator blades, direct jets of steam onto the rotor blades, causing them to turn. This spins the shaft.

What is a turbine?

For at least 2,000 years, people have used energy to power machines. The energy of flowing water turns the waterwheel. The wind blows the sails of a windmill around. Both machines have blades attached to a shaft that produces a circular, or rotary, motion. But in places where there is no wind or water, these machines cannot work. We have other machines that produce rotary motion. They are called **turbines.** Turbines are driven by steam, hot gases, wind, or water.

Steam turbines

Steam turbines can be extremely powerful machines. They can drive electric generators in power stations. In many ocean liners they are the chief power source. In most ships, the engines turn the shafts that drive the propellers.

This factory makes steam turbines for ships and electricity generators.

Gas turbines

Gas turbines are also used to generate electricity in power stations and to power locomotives. In a gas turbine, air is squeezed, or compressed, to high pressure by a fan-like device called the **compressor.** Then liquid fuel and compressed air are mixed in a combustion chamber and lit. Hot gases are given off, spinning the turbine wheels. Part of the turbine's power runs the compressor. Most of it drives the machinery.

Most jet aircraft are powered by gas turbines. Gas turbines burn a kerosene-like fuel. The burning fuel produces hot gases. The gases push out at the back of the jet, thrusting the aircraft forward.

Piston engines

Most modern machines are driven by an engine of some kind. An engine is a machine that changes energy into mechanical motion. A car engine, for example, changes the energy released by burning gasoline into motion to turn the car's wheels. Most engines use pistons to change the energy from burning fuel into mechanical energy. Gasoline, diesel, and steam are all fuels that can drive **piston engines.**

Internal combustion

Most cars use gasoline engines. A gasoline engine is one type of **internal combustion engine,** in which the fuel burns, or combusts, inside the engine. Gasoline is mixed with air inside a cylinder. This mixture is then lit by an electric spark. As the mixture burns, it produces hot gases which expand inside the cylinder and force down a piston.

What is a piston?

The **piston** is a plunger, shaped like an upside-down cup and set inside a cylinder. The piston slides up and down inside the cylinder. Hot gases from the burning fuel force the piston down. The piston is connected to the engine crankshaft and forces it to turn around. Each movement, up or down, is called a **stroke.**

Crankshaft

Most engines are used to drive wheels, which need to turn in a circle. But pistons only move up and down. So a piston engine has to change the up-and-down movement of the pistons into the circular motion needed to turn the wheels. This is done by a **crankshaft.**

The crankshaft is a long rod that has a series of bends, or cranks, along it. Each crank is connected to a piston. As the piston pushes down, it forces the crank around, somewhat like the pedal on a bicycle. The up-and-down movement is turned into a circular movement. The movement connects through gears to drive the wheels.

Inside a cylinder

Each cylinder in this piston engine works on a four-stroke cycle.

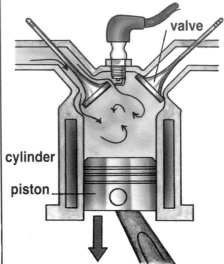

1. As the piston moves down, a fuel and air mixture is sucked into the cylinder through an open valve. The other valve remains closed.

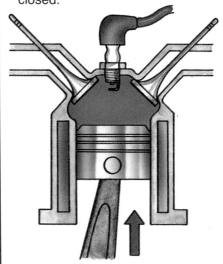

2. The piston is pushed upwards on its second stroke. Both valves are closed. The piston squeezes, or compresses, the fuel mixture into a small space in the cylinder head.

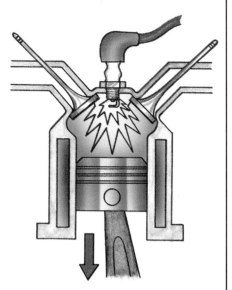

3. Then a spark from a spark plug lights the fuel mixture. The hot gases produced push the piston down on its third stroke. At the end of this stroke, the second valve opens.

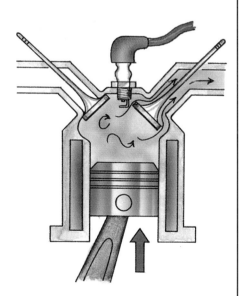

4. Then the piston comes up for its fourth stroke. It pushes the burnt gases out through the open valve and out through the car exhaust pipe. Then the valve closes. Another cycle starts when the piston moves down again.

In four strokes

Most gasoline engines work on a four-stroke cycle. On the first stroke, the cylinder sucks in a fuel mixture. On the second stroke, the piston compresses the mixture inside the cylinder. On the third stroke, the mixture explodes with a bang, forcing the piston down. On the fourth stroke, the piston moves up, blowing gases out through the exhaust pipe.

Piston engines have a number of separate cylinders. Each cylinder works on a different stroke of the cycle. In a four-cylinder engine, when cylinder one is on the first stroke, cylinder two is on the third stroke, cylinder three is on the fourth stroke and cylinder four is on the second stroke. There is always one exploding cylinder to turn the crankshaft.

Cams and camshafts

Each of the valves inside the engine's cylinders is opened and closed by an unevenly-shaped wheel, called a cam. Each cam is attached to one side of a rotating rod called the camshaft. When the cam turns, it pushes down against both the valve and a spring, opening the valve. The spring then closes the valve until the cam comes around again.

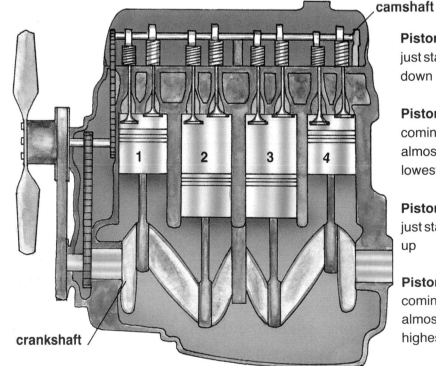

camshaft

Piston 1 — just started down

Piston 2 — coming down, almost at lowest point

Piston 3 — just started up

Piston 4 — coming up, almost at highest point

crankshaft

The automobile

The automobile is a complicated machine. It is made up of as many as 15,000 separate parts. They vary in size from the large panels that form the body to tiny ball-bearings around 1/16 of an inch (a few millimeters) in diameter. Sets of these parts work together as a group, or system, to do a certain job. And the various systems work together to make the car move.

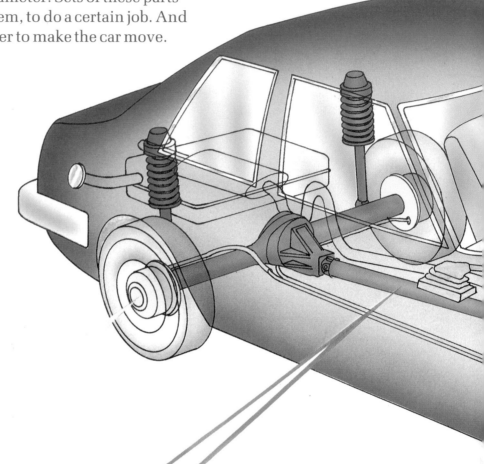

Brakes

Cars have two kinds of brakes. They usually have **disk brakes** on the front wheels and **drum brakes** at the back. In a disk brake, a steel disk is fixed to the wheel and turns with it. When a driver presses the brake pedal, hydraulic pistons force a pair of brake pads against the disk. This makes the wheel slow down. In a drum brake, curved brake shoes are forced against the inside of a drum that turns with the back wheels.

Transmission

The transmission carries power from the engine to the driving wheels of the car. A **manual transmission** includes a clutch, gears, drive shaft, and final drive. An **automatic transmission** does not require a clutch.

When a driver changes gears, the clutch pedal releases the engine from the rest of the transmission.

The gears let the car travel at different speeds. A low gear is used on a steep road or when the car is moving slowly. The drive shaft links the gears with the final drive. The final drive passes the engine power on to the driving wheels. Cars that have their driving wheels and engine at the same end have no drive shaft.

Suspension

The car's suspension allows the car to travel over bumpy roads more smoothly. On the front and back axles of the car there are springs and **shock absorbers.** Most shock absorbers consist of a piston inside a cylinder filled with oil or air. As the car wheel goes over a bump, the piston is forced up into the cylinder and the oil or air helps soften the force of the bump.

Mechanical systems

The main mechanical systems of the automobile are the **engine, transmission, brakes, steering,** and **suspension.** The car also has hydraulic, cooling, lubrication, and electrical systems. A hydraulic system works the brakes of most cars. The electrical system carries electricity to the engine, lights, and instruments. It includes a generator driven by the engine, which keeps the battery charged with electricity. The cooling system keeps the engine cool, and the lubrication system feeds oil to the moving parts.

Steering

Most cars steer with their front wheels, which are connected to a **tie-rod.** A steering column attached to the tie-rod connects it to the steering wheel inside the car.

As the driver turns the steering wheel, a small gear at the bottom of the column moves around. This pushes the tie-rod from side to side and changes the direction of the wheels.

Engine

Most car engines have four, six, or eight cylinders. Inside each cylinder is a piston.

As the pistons move up and down, they drive the crankshaft around very fast. The transmission takes this power and sends it to a drive shaft, which makes the wheels turn.

Pumping gas

If you have watched someone filling a car with gas, you may have wondered where the gas comes from. It couldn't be contained in the pump itself. The pump wouldn't hold enough gas to fill a car's tank.

The gas is stored in large underground tanks at the gas station. Huge gas tankers bring gas from oil refineries to keep the tanks filled. The gas then has to be pumped up to reach the car. But how does the gas get from the storage tank, up to the nozzle, and then into car?

What is a rotary pump?

Inside a gas pump is a machine called a **rotary pump.** The rotary pump can move liquid gas from the storage tank to the car. This is how it works. First, an electric motor is switched on to set the pump in motion. It draws gas up from the storage tank. The rotary pump has a kind of wheel called a **rotor** which is fixed slightly off-center. The rotor has slots around it fitted with blades, or **vanes,** that slide in and out of the slots. When the rotor is going around, the vanes are pushed out against the edge of the pump. The rotor isn't in the middle of the pump, so the space around the sides of the rotor is not the same size all the way around.

As the gas goes around the pump, it is squeezed into a smaller space between the rotor and the inside wall of the pump. This forces the gas out of the pump at high pressure, and it shoots up to the nozzle. When you squeeze the trigger on the nozzle, gas flows out.

gas gauge

gas

rotary pump

rotor

vane

The gas comes up from the underground tank and is pushed out of the pump at high pressure.

electric motor

gas

Measuring the flow

On its way to the nozzle, the gas passes through an **air separator.** The gas vapor and air that have collected in the tank can escape safely into the air. Then the gas flows through a gauge that measures and records the amount of gas going into the car. There is often a small computer that tabulates the cost of the gas.

So, the next time you see someone squeezing the trigger on a gas pump, think of all the different machines working together inside the pump to deliver the gas to the car.

nozzle

Reaching the fire

Fighting fires is dangerous work. Special fire-fighting machines are used to help put out fires and rescue people in danger. Fire trucks carry heavy hoses that can pump water and foam on to a fire. Ladders help the fire fighters reach the higher stories of buildings on fire.

Working the boom

Sometimes, the ladders are not tall enough to reach safely to the top of multistory buildings. Then the fire fighters have to send for the aerial ladder or elevating platform trucks. Each of these has a long arm, called a **boom,** which turns around on a turntable. At the end of the boom is a platform like a cage, where several people can stand. The boom is lifted up, taking fire fighters and firehoses closer to the burning building. A boom on the largest fire trucks can lift fire fighters and their equipment 150 feet (46 meters) into the air.

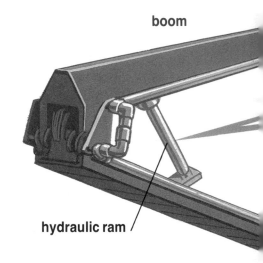

boom

hydraulic ram

Hydraulic power

What is the machine that has the power to lift the boom up so high? It's a **hydraulic** machine. This kind of hydraulic machine uses a liquid to push a piston up and down inside a cylinder. As the piston moves up or down, the boom is lifted or lowered.

A hydraulic platform can lift fire fighters up to a fire in a tall building.

Find out more by looking at pages **98–99**

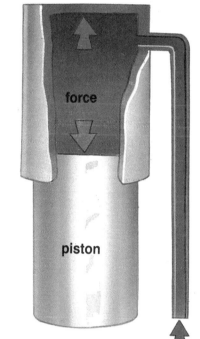

cylinder

oil

piston

force

piston

oil

How do hydraulic pistons work?

A hydraulic machine has two cylinders, a narrow, smaller cylinder and a wide, larger cylinder. Each cylinder contains a round piston that slides up and down inside it. The cylinders are filled with a liquid and are joined together by a thin pipe.

A force presses against the piston in the smaller cylinder. The piston is pushed along the narrow cylinder, which forces the liquid out, along the pipe, and into the larger cylinder, where it pushes against the wide piston. Because the larger cylinder has a larger area than the smaller cylinder, the force is stronger—powerful enough to lift the boom.

A machine that flies

For thousands of years, people dreamed of a flying machine that could carry them through the air. The first airplanes were gliders. But it was not until the engine was invented that people could build machines to take off using their own power.

Propellers

On the nose of some aircraft, you will see a **propeller.** Most airplane propellers have two or more blades. These blades are set at an angle and fixed to a shaft that is driven by the engine. Each blade is shaped like the wing of a plane. When the engine is running, the pilot can turn on the propeller. As it turns, the propeller pulls the plane forward.

How do airplanes fly?

The wings of an airplane have a very special shape. They are fairly flat underneath, round at the front, and curved on top, with a sharp edge at the back. This shape is called an **airfoil.** When air travels past an airfoil, it has to travel farther over the curved top than under the flat bottom. This means the air over the top has to travel faster. And when air travels faster, the pressure drops. The high pressure under the wing pushes upward and lifts the wing. When the plane is speeding fast enough along the runway, the wings produce enough **lift** for the plane to take off.

Controlling flight

The pilot controls an aircraft from the **cockpit** at the front of the plane. It is filled with instruments, such as the altimeter and air-speed indicator, that help the pilot stay on course. The pilot also has a control column which is linked to hinged panels on the airplane's wings and tail, called **ailerons** and **elevators.** These devices help the airplane to take off, land, and turn. A foot pedal works the **rudder,** which helps to steer the aircraft. And the **throttle** controls the speed and power of the engine.

A pilot controls the aircraft by moving a control column and foot pedals. These controls are connected to hinged flaps on the wings and tail of the plane.

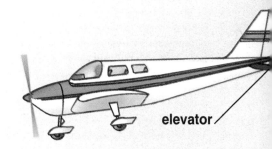

elevator

1. The engine is turned on. The pilot opens the throttle and the propeller starts to turn, slowly at first and then faster and faster. The plane moves along the runway.

propeller

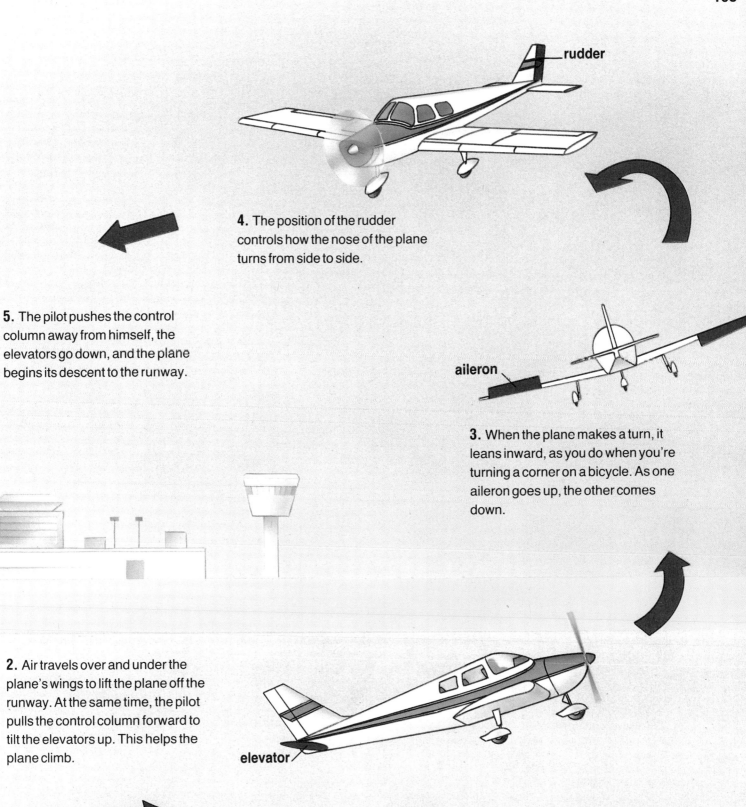

rudder

4. The position of the rudder controls how the nose of the plane turns from side to side.

5. The pilot pushes the control column away from himself, the elevators go down, and the plane begins its descent to the runway.

aileron

3. When the plane makes a turn, it leans inward, as you do when you're turning a corner on a bicycle. As one aileron goes up, the other comes down.

2. Air travels over and under the plane's wings to lift the plane off the runway. At the same time, the pilot pulls the control column forward to tilt the elevators up. This helps the plane climb.

elevator

Going up?

Have you ever been inside a modern building and wanted to go up to the 25th floor? Just think how tired you'd be if you had to climb 25 flights of stairs to get there! Of course you don't need to do this—you can use the **elevator.**

Most elevators work automatically. You summon them by pressing a button on the wall in the hallway. The elevator arrives and the doors open automatically. You get in and press the button showing the floor you want to go to. When you arrive, the doors open again to let you out.

How does an elevator work?

An elevator travels up and down inside a vertical passageway called an elevator shaft. An elevator can be powered by electricity or by a hydraulic system. Inside the shaft of an **electric traction elevator,** strong cables are attached to an elevator car. The cables run over a pulley called a **sheave,** at the top of the lift shaft. The sheave is connected to an electric motor. At the other end, the cables are attached to a very heavy weight called a **counterweight.** This counterweight is a kind of balance. The counterweight weighs about the same as the elevator car with an average number of passengers in it. So when the electric motor is switched on, it only needs to use enough power to lift the weight of extra people in the car. The rest of the weight is balanced by the counterweight. If there are few people in the elevator, the electric motor uses less power to move it up and down.

Some elevators travel as far as 400 to 2,000 feet (120 to 600 meters) in a minute. It would not take long for an elevator to reach the top floor of this shopping center in Johannesburg, South Africa.

You will need

a matchbox

a piece of string, about 7 in (18 cm) long

a cork

adhesive tape

some stiff wire

a clear plastic bottle

scissors

a heavy nut

Going down

Make this model elevator to see how pulleys and counterweights work.

1. Make a hole in one end of the matchbox. Thread the string through, and tie a knot in one end. Tie a heavy nut on the other end of the string. This is the counterweight.

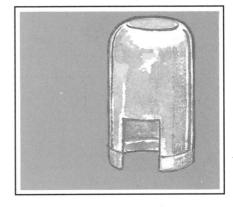

2. Ask an adult to help you cut the top off a plastic bottle. Cut a small door in the bottom. Cover the sharp edges with adhesive tape.

3. Bend one end of a length of wire into a handle shape. Ask an adult to help you push the wire through one side of the bottle. Thread the cork onto the wire, and push the wire out through the opposite side of the bottle.

4. Wind the string twice around the cork, letting the nut hang free. The matchbox is ready to lift its first load.

Electric motors

Think of some of the machines you use at home. You may have a washing machine, hairdryer, vacuum cleaner, refrigerator, sewing machine, or an electric fan. Most of the machines we use at home are driven by an electric motor. This is a machine that changes the energy in electricity into movement.

Electric motors don't burn solid or liquid fuel, so they are clean and they don't cause pollution. They can be used almost anywhere. They just need to be plugged into an electricity supply or powered by a battery. Electric motors can be very small. So they can be used to power a small machine such as an electric toothbrush.

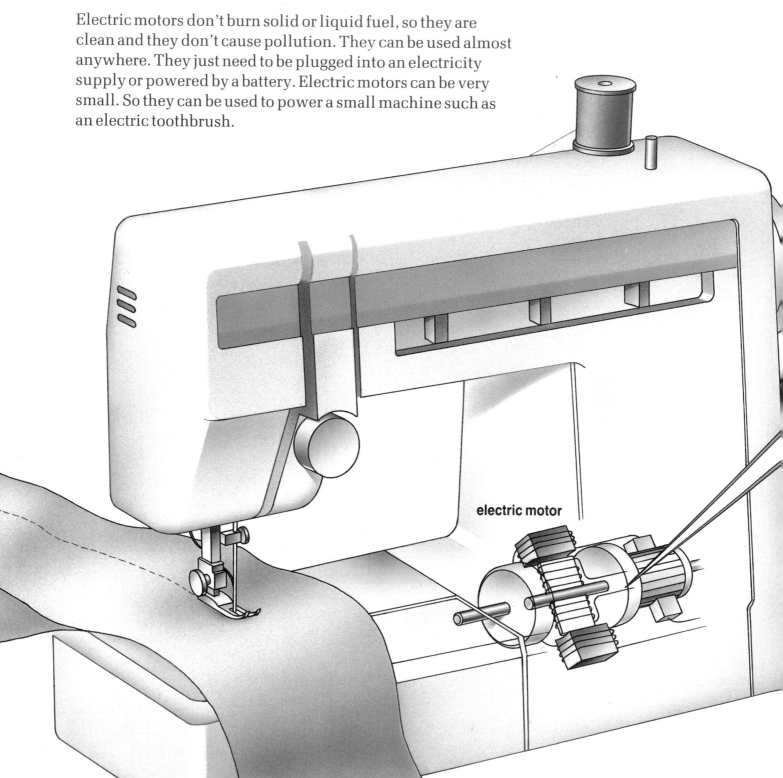

electric motor

Find out more by looking at pages **90–91**

Inside an electric motor

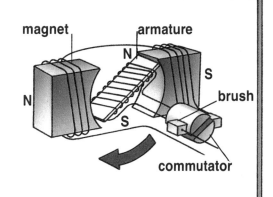
magnet · armature · brush · commutator

1. When the power is switched on, the electric current flows through the brushes to the commutator and then to the armature. The armature becomes magnetized. The north and south poles of the magnet attract the opposite poles of the armature, making the armature rotate in a clockwise direction.

2. As the armature rotates between the poles of the magnet, the commutator causes the current to reverse its direction. This, in turn, causes a reversal of the polarity of the armature. The north pole then faces the north pole of the magnet. The armature continues to rotate in an attempt to bring unlike poles together.

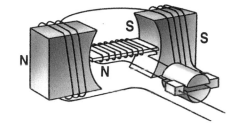

3. The poles of the magnet again repel the poles of the armature. This forces it around to its starting position. It has turned full circle. The armature spins many times per minute until the electricity is turned off.

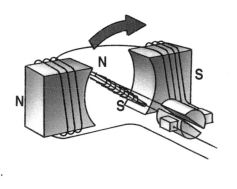

If you could see inside a sewing machine, you would find a small electric motor. It can provide enough power to raise and lower the needle.

Using magnets in motors

An electric motor changes electric energy to mechanical energy to do work. In a simplified electric motor, coils of wire are wound around a core. This is called an **armature.** The armature can rotate between two poles of a magnet. Each end of the wire is attached to a drum called a **commutator,** which is made of two split rings. An electric current is brought to the coils through carbon blocks, called **brushes,** which are in contact with the commutator. When the power is switched on, the armature becomes an electromagnet.

Printing revolution

Just imagine how long this book would have taken to produce 600 years ago! In those days, there were no engines to power machines. There weren't even any machines to print books. Virtually every book was copied by hand.

In the mid-1400's, the **printing press** was invented. Each letter of the alphabet was carved separately on a block of wood or cast in a piece of metal. The letters were backwards and had a raised surface. They were called **type.** The printer arranged the type in lines in a tray, making up words and sentences.

Pictures were also carved on blocks and fitted with the type to make up a page. Then the raised surface was inked. A piece of paper was laid on top of the inked page and a heavy weight pressed on top. When the paper was removed, the ink left an impression of the page that was no longer backwards, but the right way around. These books were almost always printed with a single color ink. So all the pictures were black and white.

Each piece of type must be put in place one by one. Early printers had to set type that they read backwards.

Speed and color

Printing presses today are huge machines, powered by electricity and controlled by computers. Photography also helps in the printing process. Words and color pictures are photographed on film. The film is used to make **printing plates.** These are fitted onto cylinders in the printing press.

Large sheets or huge rolls of paper are fed into the printing press. The machine can quickly produce thousands of identical pages in all colors. The printer operates a computer to control the speed of the press and the colors of the print.

An electronic computer scans this picture to make photographic films. These will be made into printing plates.

Machines to make machines

If you ever tried to build a machine, you would soon find out that all the parts must fit well together. Otherwise, the machine would not work properly. If the parts rub against each other, they soon wear down. Shaking, or vibrations, can loosen the nuts and screws, and the machine might fall apart.

Imagine you decide to build a model car. You need to find all the correct materials and to mark and measure them. Then you must shape the body, grind four wheels to the same size, and cut two axles to the same length. The finished model is so good that your friend asks you to make another. Now you have to start all over again finding the materials, then cutting and measuring them. It would have been quicker to have made all the parts for both cars at the same time.

Industrial tools

In industries, there are special machines, called **machine tools,** that can produce many identical parts over and over again. These machines can cut and shape metal with great accuracy, or precision.

A **saw** cuts metal to a certain size or shape. Almost every material needs to be cut.

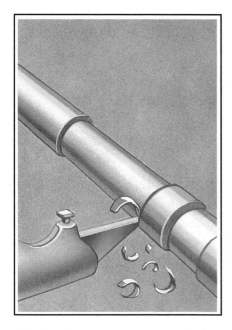

A **lathe** shaves pieces off a rotating piece of metal. This is how many parts of car engines are made.

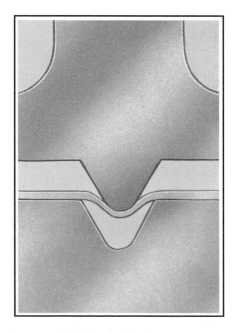

Press brakes press a sheet of metal between two shapes, or molds. This is how the body panels of cars are made.

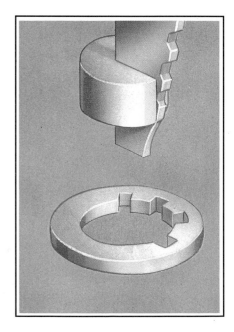

A **broach** gives a hole a special shape. Slots on the inside of car gears are made like this.

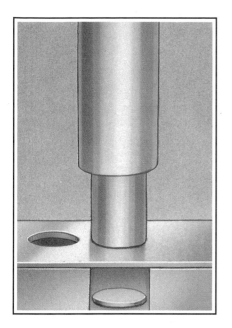

A **punch press** stamps holes into sheet metal. This is how blanks for coins are shaped.

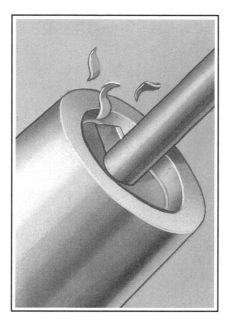

A **borer** cuts round holes and smooths them. This is how large gun barrels are made.

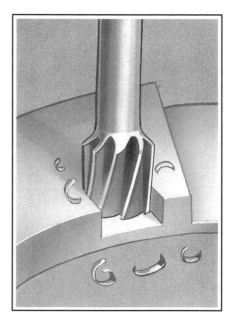

A **milling tool** cuts flat surfaces in metal. This is how gear teeth are milled.

A **grinding wheel** rubs against a surface to make it smooth. This is how drills are sharpened.

Keeping cool

When the moving parts of a machine rub against each other, heat is produced. Many machine tools become very hot while they are cutting and drilling. The cutting edge of the tool rubs against the material being shaped. This causes friction, and friction produces heat.

Often, sparks fly up from the metal cutting surface of the machine tool. The machine operators wear gloves to protect their hands and goggles to protect their eyes. The cutting tool is sprayed with an oily mixture. This oil lubricates, or oils, the cutting tool, preventing too much wear. It also carries away much of the heat caused by friction and keeps the metal from becoming too hot.

Some machine tools become so hot that they have to be made of special steel containing a metal called tungsten. Tungsten can be mixed with iron to make an alloy that stays hard and sharp even when it is very hot.

Working on the assembly line

Most of the goods we buy these days are not made individually by a skilled worker. They are put together, or assembled, step-by-step on an **assembly line.**

On an assembly line, the workers stand alongside a moving **conveyor belt.** Each person adds another part to the product as it passes by on the conveyor. Each set of parts must be identical to every other set. Otherwise, they will not fit together properly. This is where machine tools are so important — they can produce parts that are exactly right.

At each stage of the assembly line, there is one simple task to carry out. So each task can be completed quickly. Therefore, a product can be assembled much faster than it would if one person assembled the whole product. So goods can be produced in large quantities. This type of assembly is known as **mass production.**

This robot is putting a windshield onto a car. It can repeat the task many times over.

Built by robots

Machines are often used for mass production. They can carry out simple tasks swiftly and accurately. Machines that do not require human assistance to carry out physical tasks, such as spraying paint, welding, and simple assembly work, are called **robots.** The robot is first taken through each step of the task in simple movements. Each movement is recorded in its computer. The computer can then put together the instructions for these movements, in the right order. Robots do not get tired like human workers. And they can work in heat, fumes, and noise that people would find unpleasant or dangerous. Today, robots carry out many tasks that people used to do.

Today, many robots have built-in video cameras that allow them to "see" and avoid obstacles.

Robots are useful in situations where people may be injured. This robot is used by a bomb disposal team. The briefcase may conceal a bomb, so the robot is sent in to investigate. The bomb disposal team uses a remote-controlled handset to guide the robot to the briefcase from a safe distance.

You will need

thread spools or plastic 35-mm film containers with lids

a small cardboard box

a hook or a magnet

three knitting needles

modeling clay

cotton thread

wire

thick cardboard

adhesive tape

scissors

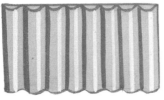

corrugated cardboard

a cork

paper fasteners

Make a robot

This cardboard robot can pick up small objects with its specially designed arms.

Caterpillar wheels

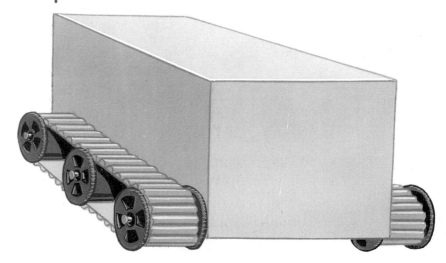

1. Push the knitting needles through the ends and the middle of the base of the box. Slide a thread spool or film container onto both ends of each needle. Secure the ends with a lump of modeling clay.

2. To make a caterpillar track, cut two strips of corrugated cardboard. They should be long enough to wind over all three sets of wheels. Use adhesive tape to join the ends of the track together.

An arm that stretches

1. Cut six short strips from a thick sheet of cardboard. The strips should be 7 inches (18 centimeters) long and 1 inch (2.5 centimeters) wide.

2. Lay the pieces of cardboard out in a criss-cross pattern and join them together with paper fasteners. Use one large paper fastener in the middle to attach the arm to the body.

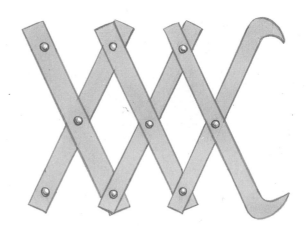

A pulley for lifting

1. Cut a hole in the back of the box, big enough to fit a thread spool. Wind thread around a spool, and tie a hook on the end.

2. Push the wire through one side of the box. Slide the thread spool onto the wire. Push the wire out the other side.

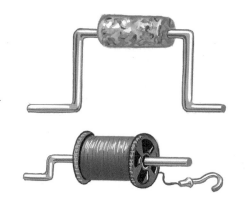

3. Bend the wire to make a handle.

4. Push some wire through the cork. Bend the wire at either side to make "legs," as shown. Tape this to the front of the box.

5. Pull the thread over the cork, with the hook hanging down, as shown.

Experiments with your robot

Collect as many objects as you can. How many of these objects can you pick up with your robot? What can you pick up with the pulley and hook? What can you pick up with the stretching arm? What would happen if you used a magnet instead of a hook?

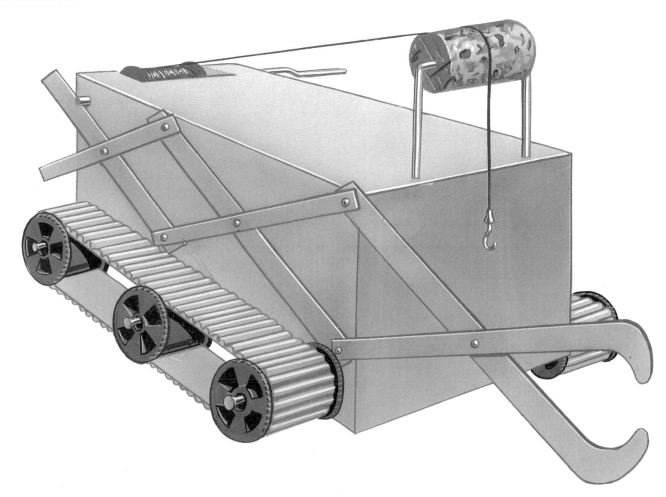

Glossary

Architect: Person who designs a building.

Assembly line: Arrangement of workers and product parts in which each worker adds a specific part to each unit.

Bridge: *Structure* that crosses water, a road, or valley, so that people can get from one side to the other.

Cement: Building material made of lime, clay, and water mixed, dried, burned, and ground to a powder.

Compact: To make solid.

Compression: A *force* that tries to crush something, or push it into itself.

Concrete: Building material made by mixing *cement,* sand, water, and small stones.

Container: Something that encloses and protects another item.

Dam: *Structure* that stops a river from flowing.

Electric motor: Engine that changes electric energy into *mechanical energy.*

Elevation: Building plan showing an outside wall.

Energy: Capacity, or ability, to do work.

Engine: *Machine* that changes energy into *mechanical motion.*

External combustion engine: *Engine* in which the fuel burns, or combusts, outside the engine.

Floor plan: Building plan showing an overhead view of each story.

Force: Energy that makes an object move or change direction.

Foundation: The base upon which a *structure* rests.

Framework: The "skeleton" of a *structure,* usually made of steel, around which the rest of the structure is built.

Friction: *Force* of rubbing between two surfaces that uses up energy by turning it to heat.

Gear: Wheel with notches, or cogs, cut around its edge.

Geodesic dome: Curved *structure* with a circular base and a dome-shaped frame made of triangles of steel rods.

Hydraulic: Operated by the movement or *force* of liquid.

Inclined plane: Simple *machine* made of a slope; it enables a small force to lift a load a long distance.

Inertia: Resistance to change.

Insulator: Anything that traps air and prevents the movement of heat.

Internal combustion engine: *Engine* in which the fuel burns, or combusts, inside the engine.

Kinetic energy: Energy of motion.

Lattice structure: *Structure* formed when horizontal and vertical sides of a metal cage are strengthened by diagonal bars.

Lever: Simple *machine* made of an arm that pivots around a support called a **fulcrum** to lift a load.

Machine: Arrangement of fixed and moving parts for doing work.

Machine tool: *Machine* that cuts and shapes metal to produce machine parts.

Mass production: Type of production that uses an *assembly line* so that goods can be produced in large quantities.

Mechanical energy: Form of *energy* that drives machines.

Mortar: Mixture of *cement,* sand, and water used to hold bricks together.

Piston engine: *Engine* that uses *pistons*—plungers that slide up and down inside a cylinder—to change energy from burning fuel into *mechanical energy.*

Potential energy: Stored *energy.*

Power: That amount of work done during a length of time.

Pressure: *Force* caused by pushing on or against something.

Prestressed concrete: *Concrete* that hardens around stretched steel cables, which are then released, compressing the concrete.

Properties: Qualities or characteristics of a material.

Pulley: Simple *machine* made of a wheel turning on an axis and a rope moving in a groove around the wheel's rim. It changes a *force's* direction.

Reinforced steel: Sheets of steel strengthened by the addition of extra pieces of metal.

Reinforced concrete: *Concrete* beams strengthened with steel rods or bars.

Reservoir: Body of water created behind a dam.

Robot: Computerized *machine* that carries out physical tasks without human help.

Rolling: Process in steelmaking in which red-hot steel is squeezed between rollers into shapes designed to give strength.

Scale drawing, Scale model: Drawing or model that shows a *structure* in reduced size, with parts in the same proportion to each other as in finished building.

Skyscraper: Building with many floors supported by a steel framework.

Structural engineer: Person who designs the framework of a *structure* and decides how the engineering problems are to be solved.

Structure: Object built of one or more materials, either natural or artificial, to enclose or support something or to span a space.

Tensile strength: Ability to withstand *forces* of *tension.*

Tension: *Force* that tries to pull something apart.

Turbine: *Machine* that produces *rotary motion,* spinning a shaft.

Wedge: Simple *machine* made of two inclined planes back to back; it changes the direction of a *force* and increases it.

Wheel and axle: Simple *machine* made of one or more wheels turning on a rod called an *axle.*

Work: Measure of the effort, or *force,* used to move an object over a distance.

Index

A

action [piano], 76
aerial ladder, 102
aileron, 104–105
airfoil, 104
airplane, 10, 12, 95, 104–105
air separator, 101
air-speed indicator, 104
altimeter, 104
amplifier, 76
aqueduct, 9, 34
arch bridge, 35
arch dam, 50–51
architecture, 30–31, 60–61
arm, 72
armature, 109
asphalt, 52
assembly line, 114–115
automatic transmission, 98
automobile, 65, 98–99
    mechanical system, 99
axe, 79
axle, 65, 82–83, 87
Aztecs, 28, 31

B

Babylonians, 28, 35
badger, 8
ball-bearings, 71
battery, 99
bench, 9
bicycle, 67, 71, 86–87
Big Boys [locomotive], 93
Biosphere II, 60–61
bird, 58
blacktop, 52
block and tackle, 89
boiler, 92
bolt, 80–81
bomb disposal team, 115
boom, 102–103
bore, 32
borer, 113

box girder bridge, 35
brace and bit, 83
brakes, 86–87, 98
Brazil, 42
brick, 20–21
bridge, 9, 12, 34–37, 52–53
Britain, 28
broach, 112
brush [electromagnet], 109
Buddhism, 31
bulldozer, 28
burrow, 8
buttress, 25
buttress dam, 50–51

C

cable, 17, 23, 39, 40, 54, 106
cable-stayed bridge, 36–37
cage, 39
cam, 97
cambered road, 55
camshaft, 97
cantilever bridge, 37
Capitol, 48
catapult, 74–75
caterpillar wheels, 116
cement, 22
chainwheel, 87
Channel Tunnel, 46–47
Chicago, 42
Chichimec Indians, 31
chimney, 92, 93
Chinese, 31, 42
cladding, 42
clay, 20, 22
climate, 60–61
clinker, 22
clock, 65, 69, 82, 84–85
clockwork mechanisms, 84–85
clothing, 14
clutch, 98
cockpit, 104
cog, 83, 84–85
coil, 109

commutator, 109
compacting machine, 52
compressor, 95
compression, 16–17, 22–23, 27, 96
computer, 111
concrete, 12–13, 19, 22–23, 42
   prestressed, 23
   reinforced, 23
cone, 10
container, 14–15
control column, 104–105
conveyor belt, 114–115
copper, 26
core, 32, 42
cotton, 12–13
counterweight, 106–107
crane, 9, 28, 39, 88–89
crank, 87
crankshaft, 96, 97, 99
crossbeam, 74
cube, 10
cylinder, 10, 92, 93, 96, 97, 99, 103

D

damper [piano], 76
dampness. see **moisture**
damp proofing, 57
dams, 50–51
dandelion, 8
deck, 40
Delhi, India, 18
desert, 61
design, 30–31
diesel, 96
disk brakes, 98
distance, 67
dome, 48–49
drainage system, 46
drill, 83
drive shaft, 98
drum brakes, 98

E

earthworm, 8
effort, 67, 79
Egyptians, 28
Eiffel Tower, 38
electricity, 50, 67, 95
electric motor, 65, 108–109
electric traction elevator, 106
electromagnet, 109
elevation, 31
elevator, 106–107
elevator [aircraft], 105
elevator shaft, 106
embankment dam, 50–51
energy, 67, 90–91, 94–95
engine, 99, 104
engineering, 30–31, 42, 50–51, 52–53, 60–61
escapement, 84–85
excavator, 28
exhaust, 93, 97
expressways, 52–53
external combustion engine, 93

F

face shield, 14
farmland, 61
feather, 58
fiberglass, 14, 19
fire, 26
firebox, 93
fire fighting, 102–103
fire hose, 102
fire truck, 102
first-class lever, 72
Firth of Forth railway bridge, 37
floor plan, 31
football, 68
football player, 14
foot pedal, 77, 104
force, 17, 67, 68
foundation, 32–33, 42
framework, 26

France, 28, 46–47
freeways, 52–53
friction, 67, 70, 71, 87, 113
fuel, 65, 67, 93, 95, 96–97
fulcrum, 72
Fuller, Richard Buckminster, 49

G

gasoline, 65, 67, 96
   pumping, 100–101
gas system, 54–55
gas turbine, 95
gear, 65, 83, 84, 86, 98
generator, 90, 94, 99
geodesic dome, 49
girder, 27
girder bridge, 35
Gladesville Bridge, 23
glass, 12–13, 19
glider, 104–105
gloves, 14
glue, 22
grand piano, 76–77
gravity, 69, 70
Great Britain, 46–47, 52–53
Great Stupa, 31
Great Wall, 31
grinding wheel, 113

H

hammer [piano], 76
Hampton Court, 21
heat, 26, 58–59, 67, 71, 113
helmet, 14
hexagonal nut, 80
hockey player, 14
Hong Kong, 42–43
house, 9
household appliance, 108–109
hydraulic piston, 103
hydraulic power, 102–103, 106
hydroelectricity, 50

I

ice, 70
inclined plane, 65, 78
India, 31, 48
inertia, 69
insulation, 58–59
internal combustion engine, 92–93, 96
iron, 26

J

jack, 81
jacket [platform], 40
jackscrew, 81
Johannesburg, South Africa, 106
junction, 52–53

K

keyboard [piano], 76
kinetic energy, 90

L

ladder, 102
lamppost, 9, 44
lathe, 112
lattice, 38–39
lattice tower, 39
Leaning Tower of Pisa, 33
leather, 12–13
leg pad, 14
lever, 65, 72, 76–77
lift [aircraft], 104
lighthouse, 45
lime, 22
locomotive, 92–93, 95
lubrication, 71, 113

M

machine, 65, 67, 74–75. *see also specific types*
machine tools, 112–113
magnet, 109

Mahesana Junction, India, 92–93
Malaysia, 34
manhole, 55
manual transmission, 98
mass production, 114–115
material, 8, 12–13, 15
    artificial, 12–13
    building, 18–19
    modern, 19
    natural, 12–13
    properties, 12
mat foundation, 32
mathematics, 73
mechanical advantage, 73, 80–81, 89
mechanical energy, 90–91
Melbourne, Australia, 30
metal plate, 55
Mexico, 28, 31
milling tool, 113
model, 30–31
moisture, 56–57
mortar, 22
mountain, 79

N

nautilus shell, 25
nest, 8
Newcastle University, 49
New York, 42
New York Harbor, 36
Nile River, 35
nut, 80–81

O

ocean, 61
ocean liner, 94
oil [lubrication], 113
oil platform, 40–41
Omdurman, Sudan, 35
overpass, 52–53

P

Paris Exhibition of 1889, 38
pedal, 67, 77, 104
pendulum clock, 84
perpetual movement, 66
Philippines, 49
photography, 111
piano, 76–77
pier, 34
pier foundation, 32
pile-driver, 28
pile foundation, 32
pillar, 9
pipe, 54
piston, 90, 92, 93, 96–97, 99, 103
piston engine, 96–97
pitch, 81
plane, 78
plank, 78
plans, 30–31
plastic, 12–13, 19
platform, 40–41
pneumatic, 86
Pont du Gard, 34
population, 60–61
potential energy, 90
power, 67. see also **energy**
power station, 94, 95
press brake, 112
pressure, 50
printing, 110–111
printing plate, 111
printing press, 110–111
propeller, 94, 104
properties, 12
proportion, 30–31
protective clothing, 14, 113
pulley, 65, 88–89, 106–107, 117
pulling, 68
pump, 100–101
pumping station, 91
punch press, 113

pushing, 68
pylon, 39
pyramid, 28–29

R

racing driver, 14
radio mast, 39
raft foundation, 32
railway bridge, 9
rain, 56
rain forest, 61
ramps, 28
reinforcing, 24–25
reservoir, 50–51
resistance, 69
road base, 53
roads, 52–53, 79
   layers, 53
road subgrade, 53
road surface, 53
robot, 114–117
rolling, 27
Romans, 22, 34, 35
roof, 56
root, 8
rotary pump, 100–101
rotor, 100
rudder, 104–105
runway, 104
rust, 26

S

sand, 22
São Paulo, 42
saw, 112
scaffold, 9
scale drawing, 30–31
scale model, 30–31
Scotland, 37
screw, 65, 80–81
screwdriver, 83
seabed, 40, 46

second-class lever, 72
seesaw, 72
semisubmersible platform, 40
sewer, 55
sewing machine, 65, 109
shaft, 94
shale, 20
sheave, 106
sheet, 10
shell, 8, 25
shellfish, 8
shock absorbers, 98
skyscraper, 26, 42–43
snail, 8
snow, 56
space rocket, 45
Spaghetti junction, 52–53
span bridge, 34
spark plug, 97
sphere, 10
spiral slide, 45
spoon, 72
spring, 65, 85, 98
spring-driven clock, 85
sprocket, 86
stainless steel, 26
staircase, 25
Statue of Liberty, 26, 27
steam, 56, 57, 90–91, 92–93, 96
steamboat, 91
steam engine, 90–91, 92–93
steam turbine, 94
   factory, 95
steel, 12–13, 19, 26, 42, 113
steering, 87, 99
stone, 12–13, 18
stone, circles of, 28
Stonehenge, 31
strain, 22–23
string [piano], 76
stroke [piston], 96–97
structural engineering, 30–31

structure, 8–9
   ancient, 28–29
   containing, 14–15
   enclosing, 8
   of the future, 60–61
   natural, 8
   reinforcing, 24–25
   shapes, 10–11
   spanning, 8
   stone, 18
   supporting, 8
   wood, 18
suspension, 86, 98
suspension bridge, 36–37
Sydney, Australia, 23

T

Taj Mahal, 48–49
temperature, 58–59
tensile strength, 16–17
tension, 16–17, 22–23, 27
tent, 9
Teotihyacán, 31
third-class lever, 72
thread, 80–81
throttle, 104
tie-rod, 99
tire, 81
Tokyo, 42
tower, 38–39, 44–45
tower crane, 28
tractor, 82
train, 92–93
transmission, 86, 98, 99
tree, 8, 10–11
trench-digger, 28
triangle, 39
tug-of-war, 16–17
tugs, 40
tungsten, 113
tunnel, 9, 46–47, 54
   blasting, 47
   boring, 47
   cut and cover, 47

turbine, 90, 94–95
type [printing], 110

U

underground, 54–55

V

valve, 92, 96
valve box, 55
vane [gasoline], 100
vapor, 56
ventilation, 46
Verrazano Narrows suspension bridge, 36
vibration, 76–77
video camera, 115

W

wall, 9, 20–21, 33
water
   as energy, 94. see also steam
water level, 57
water system, 54–55
waterwheel, 94
web, 8
wedge, 65, 79
weight, 65
weight-driven clock, 84
West Indies, 19
wheel, 65, 82–83, 84, 87, 92–93, 99
wheelbarrow, 72, 78
wind, 42
   as energy, 94
windmill, 94
wing [aircraft], 104–105
wood, 12–13, 18
   splitting, 79
woodland, 61
work, 67, 79
wrench, 80, 83

Z

ziggurat, 28

126 Acknowledgements

The publishers of **World Book's Young Scientist** acknowledge the following photographers, publishers, agencies and corporations for photographs used in this volume.

Cover E. Chalker (Spectrum Colour Library); David Parker, 600 Group Fanuc (Science Photo Library)
14/15 Spectrum Colour Library
16/17 Client: Fleetguard (Cummins); Architect: Richard Rogers; Consulting Engineer: Ove Arup & Partners
18/19 ZEFA Picture Library; Spectrum Colour Library; Eich. Zingel (ZEFA Picture Library)
20/21 Spectrum Colour Library
22/23 The Photographic Library of Australia Pty Ltd
26/27 Spectrum Colour Library; ZEFA Picture Library
30/31 ZEFA Picture Library
32/33 Streichan (ZEFA Picture Library)
34/35 D. & J. Heaton (Spectrum Colour Library); Jil Paul (Hutchison Library); Hutchison Library
36/37 E. Chalker (Spectrum Colour Library); Norman Tomalin (Bruce Coleman Ltd)

38/39 Spectrum Colour Library
40/41 Spectrum Colour Library; ZEFA Picture Library
42/43 Spectrum Colour Library
48/49 Dr David Jones (Science Photo Library)
50/51 Spectrum Colour Library
52/53 Spectrum Colour Library
58/59 Spectrum Colour Library
64/65 Michael Freeman (Bruce Coleman Ltd)
68/69 Sporting Pictures UK Ltd
78/79 ZEFA Picture Library
88/90 ZEFA Picture Library
92/93 Hugh Ballantyne (ZEFA Picture Library)
94/95 ZEFA Picture Library
106/107 ZEFA Picture Library
110/111 Charles Henneghein (Bruce Coleman Ltd); Malcolm Fielding and Johnson Matthes (Science Photo Library)
114/115 Spectrum Colour Library; Science Photo Library

Illustrated by

Martin Aitchison
Martyn Andrews
Sue Barclay
Richard Berridge
Maggie Brand
Bristol Illustrators
Colin Brown
Marie DeJohn
Farley, White and Veal
Kathie Kelleher
John Lobban
Louise Martin
Jeremy Pyke
Trevor Ridley
Gary Slater
Gwen Tourret
Peter Visscher
Matthew White